Benchmarking for School Impro

In education, benchmarking is a term used to describe a method whereby a school's performance is measured against a national or localised average. This is not the sense in which the process has been used to great effect in the commercial sector, where benchmarking is a comparison against the *best*, not against the *rest*. In this, the first book to consider this form of benchmarking in an educational context, Anthony Kelly argues that measuring effectiveness against a notional median performance, as opposed to against another organisation which is acknowledged to be effective, is counterproductive.

Benchmarking for School Improvement develops comparative benchmarking as a tool for self-assessment in schools and colleges. It is a step-by-step guide to forming profitable partnerships with other organisations and is based upon what national and international school effectiveness research tells us makes for a successful school. It is a practical guide to 'doing' benchmarking, linking the process to target setting as a means of being able to gauge self-improvement.

The book covers:

- The importance of critical, as opposed to functional, processes
- Mapping and prioritisation
- Forming a consortium
- A code of practice for school benchmarking partnerships
- Collection and use of data for effective comparison
- Introduction and maintenance of quality systems in organisations
- Notions of wastage, inspection, involvement and reward
- The shifting location of value in networks
- Suggested benchmarking tables for comparing performance

Anthony Kelly works at the University of Cambridge School of Education. He was formerly a secondary school headteacher in the border region of Ireland where he pioneered a new model of school governance and cross-sector integration. He has researched widely in schools and colleges in the UK and has written extensively on organisational improvement and the application of mathematical and business models to not-for-profit decision making.

Benchmarking for School Improvement

A practical guide for comparing and achieving effectiveness

Anthony Kelly

London and New York

First published 2001 by RoutledgeFalmer
11 New Fetter Lane, London EC4P 4EE

Simultaneously published in the USA and Canada
by RoutledgeFalmer
29 West 35th Street, New York, NY 10001

RoutledgeFalmer is an imprint of the Taylor & Francis Group

© 2001 Anthony Kelly

Typeset in Times by
BOOK NOW Ltd
Printed and bound in Great Britain by
TJ International Ltd, Padstow, Cornwall

British Library Cataloguing in Publication Data
A catalogue record for this book is available from the British Library

Library of Congress Cataloging-in-Publication Data
A catalog record for this book has been requested

ISBN 0–415–25666–6

Contents

Tables

Figures

x *Figures*

Charts

Preface

This book attempts to introduce a new form of benchmarking to education – *comparative* benchmarking. It is intended for use in both secondary schools and Further Education colleges and it is hoped will encourage greater cross-sector cooperation. It is intended as a practical book and a conscious attempt has been made to keep to the essentials.

Numerous charts have been included, not in any attempt to be prescriptive or didactic, but to facilitate those who will want to initiate benchmarking without having to start from scratch. They differentiate between input, process, output and consequence targets in each of seven major areas:

- Managing the curriculum and teaching
- Discipline
- Leadership
- Managing personnel and staff development
- Managing external and customer relations
- Managing the built environment
- Managing finance.

The charts are based on what school effectiveness research – the 'hunt for the unicorn', as MacBeath (1999) calls it – tells us makes for a successful school. Although the charts have been trialled in a number of schools and are research-based, they are intended only as guides. They can and should be re-contextualised as required.

Comparison charts for benchmarking, across a maximum of three organisations, are contained in the Appendix. For the sake of consistency, they use the same seven categories and again, are intended only as guides.

Unavoidably, some of the charts use terminology peculiar to one or other sector, though they have obvious salience in both (e.g. Headteacher, principal, vocational tutor, teacher, deputy, etc.). Hopefully, readers will find the need to 'translate' from one terminology to another worth the effort.

Tony Kelly
University of Cambridge

1 Introduction to benchmarking and effectiveness

Introduction to benchmarking

Benchmarking is the analysis and comparison of performance across organisations or parts of an organisation, with a view to improvement. Individuals and organisations have always sought to improve their performance by studying what others did – it is good practice and is done all the time in the commercial sector.

There are two types of benchmarking. One relies on a comparison of outcomes against an average statistical attainment; the other on a comparison of critical processes against those in another organisation acknowledged to be more effective. Unfortunately, the term is used rather loosely to describe all manner of comparisons, without much effort being made to distinguish between the two. Unlike the commercial sector, government organisations in education espouse the 'statistical' type and naturally, most schools and colleges have come to think of benchmarking in similar terms.

Schools and colleges have therefore neglected business-type benchmarking, due partly to this lack of promotion and partly to a suspicion that business methods are not easily transferred to an education paradigm. This latter concern is legitimate, of course – some practices *are* specific to their business context – yet others are transferable. Comparative benchmarking is one such case and this book is an attempt to facilitate its transfer to education from a business setting, where it has a long and distinguished history of initiating and sustaining improvement.

The benchmarking story starts in 1959, when Xerox invented the first plain paper copier. The company became synonymous with photocopying until the mid-1970s, when a number of important patents ran out and Xerox's market share plunged. The company found itself squeezed between Japanese firms operating at the cheap end of the market and IBM at the other. Analysis revealed a large disparity in effectiveness between Xerox's different subsidiary companies and in response, the company developed an internal benchmarking system for its manufacturing, administrative and support processes. Benchmarking became the main agency for a change that eventually saw the company recapture more than one-third of the market it had lost (Zairi, 1996).

The well-publicised success of Xerox, coupled with the modern necessity to focus on process, has added further impetus to benchmarking as a modern quality management tool. In the intervening years, it has revolutionised business culture by focusing on how critical functions are best performed and how effectiveness comes about. It has encouraged change through partnership and has moved the focus away from the organisation itself, towards the customer and the competitor.

The DfEE and Ofsted, on the other hand, advocate an approach to benchmarking based on the statistical comparison of different schools with similar socio-economic characteristics. Upper quartile figures represent the standards which the best performing schools are achieving and the median sets the benchmark for under-performers in the group (QCA, 1997). This education view of benchmarking differs in five important ways from the comparative-type benchmarking it attempts to emulate.

First, comparative benchmarking focuses on the analysis and comparison of process, not output. This reflects a belief that the key to improvement lies in understanding how critical functions are best performed, rather than simply measuring outcomes. Statistical benchmarking, on the other hand, is firmly focused on the reverse, i.e. on *what* is achieved, rather than *how* it is achieved, and runs contrary to what is believed makes for effectiveness in the business sector. In focusing on output rather than process, it shifts the focus of responsibility one step away from those who carry out the essential work. Whereas processes can be planned, outcomes can only be hoped for. So statistical benchmarking denigrates strategic planning as a tool of headship and distracts attention away from those whose performance can make a difference. It is a form of quality control, when what is needed is quality assurance.

Second, comparative benchmarking is conducted by a partnership making performance comparisons between one organisation which aspires to improve and another whose practice is acknowledged to be excellent. It is not a comparison with a statistical quartile or confined to organisations who share similar markets. Statistical benchmarking, on the other hand, only serves to encourage schools towards a median performance and, in a normative way, guarantees that there will always be failing schools, no matter how effective they might be. Put simply, there will always be 25 per cent in the lower quartile!

Third, underlying the statistical view of benchmarking is the failure to separate the constituent critical processes that contribute to overall effectiveness, from the overall performance itself. It is too simplistic. It regards the school as a single organic entity, whereas, in reality, it is a network of sometimes conflicting and sometimes cooperating professionals. Critical processes need to be identified if a cycle of improvement is to be supported in schools. Comparative benchmarking does that because it focuses on critical processes, but the type of benchmarking currently recommended in education does not. How can effective performance be replicated if no one understands how it comes about?

Fourth, an unfortunate side effect of statistical benchmarking is that it discourages partnership. It pits school against school and encourages isolationism, since effective schools are only judged successful if others are judged failures. In statistical benchmarking, an effective school helping a less effective one guarantees only to threaten its own position by being hauled back towards the median.

Fifth, and finally, statistical benchmarking encourages schools to benchmark only against other schools operating in similar socio-economic circumstances. This seems contradictory in that it suggests that socio-economic circumstance is the major determinant of pupil achievement, while at the same time acknowledging that there is a wide range of achievement within any catchment. At any rate, schools operating in very similar circumstances are likely to share many common approaches in their day-to-day operation and benchmarking between such very similar organisations is unlikely to result in any great improvement. It seems more likely to encourage inertia, if anything.

Comparative benchmarking is a proven quality tool in business. It was a success for the Xerox Corporation and for thousands of other profitable companies. The government wants benchmarking to bring similar benefits to schools and colleges, but as a consequence of the shortcomings listed above, has failed to translate the essence of business benchmarking to its new environment. Statistical benchmarking is a poor surrogate. It focuses on output; quality controlling what is achieved without understanding how it comes about. It encourages inertia, discourages partnership and keeps the focus inward on the organisation.

Introduction to effectiveness

Whereas a business can measure its effectiveness by reference to the profits it makes or fails to make, a school or college is a more difficult enterprise in which to gauge the extent to which the institution has achieved its aims. The distinction between for-profit and not-for-profit organisations is most obvious when it comes to measuring effectiveness. The free market links the interests of the organisation with those of the customer and the shareholder in such a way that the business does not prosper (or even survive) unless the interests of both are served (Scott, 1997). In such an environment, effectiveness is largely determined by customers.

Not-for-profit organisations, on the other hand, lack clear-cut market-driven measurements of effectiveness, due to the absence of a customer-controlled free market. It is more difficult to select criteria for setting standards and it is more difficult to select indicators for evaluating performance in the absence of such a market, but it is not impossible.

In theory at least, there are many ways in which a school can measure its effectiveness, some manifestations of which are more easily measured than others. These manifestations fall into two categories: those that are apparent and measurable; and those that are latent or more subtle. The relative importance of the two categories is a matter of some disagreement among practitioners and academics. Benchmarking does not engage in this dispute. It takes measurable indicators of effectiveness in one institution and compares them with like measurements in another. It does not purport to compare that which cannot reasonably be measured.

The fundamental assumption made in relation to all measures of effectiveness, crude or otherwise, is that success (or effectiveness) is taken as a reflection of something being done well within the institution. However, this link between good practice and effectiveness is largely one of definition, since good practice is defined as practice that results in greater effectiveness! Therefore, effectiveness has come to be regarded as a planned result, rather than an accidental outcome, and it is this which sustains the belief that it can be analysed within and across institutions and shared among practitioners.

Benchmarking is a process which involves making comparisons within an organisation or with another organisation. Using similar points of reference, benchmarking involves examining the critical activities of one institution and comparing its performance in critical areas with the performance of another institution. The purpose is to improve performance and therefore increase effectiveness. Since institutions are continuously changing, benchmarking is a continuous process, rather than a once-off comparison with a competitor.

Benchmarking is not just about researching what another institution does. It seeks to make contemporaneous comparisons in specific areas – an outcome more easily achieved in today's information age than was the case in the past. Society is moving inexorably towards a state of perfect and complete information, where not only is information more extensive and more readily available, but is in real time and instantaneous. All organisations must have the willingness and the expertise to access this information and use it.

The greatest obstacle to benchmarking is the secrecy with which institutions operate in a competitive environment. This is no less true for schools and colleges than it is for private sector businesses. For this reason, one of the essential steps to successful external benchmarking is to find a suitable partner institution. Fortunately, this is not so problematic in the education sector, since institutions outside a small and well-defined catchment area cannot really be said to be in competition with each other. Organisations in the for-profit sector, on the other hand, generally compete without regard to geographical location, making it more difficult to find partner institutions for bench-marking.

Another obstacle to benchmarking is corporate inertia, particularly in schools and colleges unused to managing change or operating responsively to extraneous factors. Historically, schools and colleges have had a major change cycle only every 10 or 20 years, although this has shortened considerably in recent times, and the period between reform and implementation for schools has largely been governed by the time it takes legislation to go through the various stages of enactment. There is no corresponding inertia period in the for-profit sector; organisations must respond to the market immediately.

As with other innovations, benchmarking requires the support of senior managers if it is to be successful. The essence of good benchmarking is the identification of critical processes and this cannot be achieved by a 'hero innovator' working without senior management cooperation.

While benchmarking in manufacturing and service sector businesses is well established, the process is little understood or used in schools and colleges, and as already mentioned, where the term is used, it is used in a different sense (Gann, 1999). Schools and colleges are complex organisations with many different ways of measuring effectiveness. Those most easily measured include examination success, inspection reports, enrolment trends, exclusion rates and so on. It is more difficult to compare measurements of other aspects of school life such as parental perception, pastoral care effectiveness and the professional satisfaction of staff. Yet all these manifestations are assumed to be worth measuring because they are believed to reflect fundamental processes essential to what is believed makes for good practice: good quality and consistent teaching, pro-active management, institutional responsiveness, caring discipline, on-going professional development and the like.

Comparative benchmarking between organisations must involve direct contact. Sufficient current information can never be got from archives, journals or inspections. Archives may be years out of date – academic journals have a delay of at least a few months before publication – and inspection systems, such as Ofsted, are necessarily contextualised in time and circumstance. Direct contact must be established between partner organisations and maintained over the course of the benchmarking process, to ensure that only contemporaneous information is used to inform the comparison. Also, particular circumstances do influence practice within organisations, particularly in the case of schools and Further Education colleges, and only a direct exchange of information between partners can contextualise any success or failure they may have had.

Types of benchmarking

There are four main types of benchmarking:

- External competitive benchmarking;
- External non-competitive benchmarking;
- Internal benchmarking;
- Benchmarking against a 'market' leader.

Each type has different resourcing and staffing requirements. None of the four is a quick fix, although some are more 'basic' than others.

External competitive benchmarking

External competitive benchmarking involves comparison with a competitor that is perceived to be more effective, operating in a similar market place and under similar circumstances. In the education sector, if such an institution were to be in the same geographical catchment area, then it is unlikely that a partnership would be formed and vital specific information about the competitor's critical processes would only be gleaned from the transfer of staff from one institution to the other, or from accounts in professional journals (for example, Jackson, 2000). It is also unlikely that personal visits to the competitor institution would be very informative, although they could possibly reveal how far advanced the competitor actually is.

External non-competitive benchmarking

Comparison with other organisations *not* in direct competition is likely to be more productive. In the case of educational institutions, this could involve (or result in) a partnership between two or more schools from different catchment areas, or a school and a Further Education college in the same catchment area. In a broader sense, a school or college may even wish to compare some of its critical processes with those of non-educational organisations, such as public relations firms, hospital trusts and recruitment agencies. However, before this could be done, critical processes within the school or college would have to be matched, in isolation, to similar processes in the partnering organisation and an overall perspective is seldom gained. Non-competitive benchmarking is sometimes referred to as 'functional' or 'process' benchmarking.

Internal benchmarking

Benchmarking need not involve a comparison with another institution at all. It can be carried out internally, in which case similar processes are compared in terms of their effectiveness and efficiency. Most benchmarking starts with just such an internal comparison and only becomes external at a later stage, so it is a popular starting point for organisations.

Internal benchmarking is relatively straightforward in a school or college setting, although it is clearly limited by the small number of critical processes which can be compared. For example, examination results in similar subjects (with similar student intakes) can be compared in-house, but retention or exclusion rates and enrolment trends clearly cannot. Internal benchmarking is also limited by the fact that critical processes within a given organisation tend towards a 'median' way of doing things – a house style – which may be both a cause and an effect of institutional inertia, and militate against meaningful comparisons being made.

Leader benchmarking

Leader benchmarking is a comparison with another organisation whose reputation is such that it is widely recognised as a centre of outstanding practice. In all probability, such leading institutions will be non-competitor, but have little incentive to form a partnership with an institution with markedly inferior practice. Market leaders are more likely to benchmark themselves against other leading institutions outside the sector. For example, leading beacon schools and Further Education colleges sometimes benchmark themselves (informally) against successful private sector businesses or higher education institutions. However, notwithstanding the lack of incentive, leading educational institutions do tend to share practice quite readily with non-competitors, but whether this is specific or continuous enough to enable an inferior institution to benchmark, is doubtful.

Summary

- As an introduction to benchmarking, this chapter elucidated five major differences between comparative and statistical benchmarking:

  - concentration on process rather than output;
  - comparison with a partnering organisation rather than against a quartile;
  - differentiation between critical processes rather than a holistic approach;
  - the primacy of partnership over individuality;
  - encouragement of change as opposed to inertia.

- The chapter also examined the similarities and differences between measuring effectiveness in commercial and educational organisations, and outlined briefly the four basic types of benchmarking suitable for use in a school setting:

  - external competitive;
  - external non-competitive;
  - internal;
  - benchmarking against a market leader.

2 Critical processes

Why and what to benchmark

Rationale

It has been said that the strategic aim of any organisation is to survive first and to thrive second. Of course, much depends on the stage of development or maturity of the organisation and educational institutions are no different from business ones in this respect. Schools and colleges at a 'primitive' stage of development, recovering from setbacks or in special measures, may be more interested in surviving than thriving. Nevertheless, an examination of critical organisational processes can hold the key to both survival and success. Comparative benchmarking does this and more. The essence of benchmarking is that the organisation aspires to improvement, no matter how primitive or advanced its stage of development. A school or college merely interested in survival or maintaining its effectiveness, rather than improving it, will have little use for benchmarking of whatever type.

When comparative benchmarking focuses on competitive performance, it is a systematic examination of what makes a competitor, internal or external, more effective. In comparing processes across or within institutions, internal standards can be set, safe in the knowledge that they are reconciled to standards already regarded as among the best in the sector. For schools and colleges, benchmarking creates an imaginary market place where comparisons can be made between institutions not usually in competition with each other. Comparative benchmarking is learning from a leader in the field. It is about the search and rapid transfer of best practice, with a view to continuous improvement.

Since the measurement of effectiveness can be dependent on factors such as institutional size, environment, circumstance and history, it is easier to benchmark within institutions than across them. However, if external benchmarking is necessary or desirable, it is better to compare only certain organisational processes. In this way, organisations can be compared even when they are not equal in size, circumstance or sector. Schools and colleges, from both state and private sectors, can partner each other, or find benchmarking partners from outside education where only one or two particular processes are compatible. For example, the efficiency of payroll arrangements in a supermarket may usefully be compared to those in a Further Education college, but the comparison of other measures of effectiveness is unlikely to be meaningful.

Comparative benchmarking has the added advantage of structuring change within an organisation in such a way as to allow it to be tested before being put in place. Changes in work practices instituted as a result of non-competitive external benchmarking have the advantage of having been tried and tested successfully elsewhere. This is particularly important for schools and colleges, which often need to be so watchful of their immediate obligations that they neglect to change at all. Yet it would be a mistake to regard comparative benchmarking as simply institutional plagiarism. Rather it is institutional mentoring, where both 'teacher' and 'learner' organisations learn from an open exchange of information and experience. Anyway, only some processes lend themselves to comparison and suggested improvements in practice are usually specialised and elemental. Consequently, the opportunity to adopt another organisation's entire set of processes wholesale rarely presents itself.

The notion of benchmarking was developed by Robert Camp some 30 years ago in an attempt to halt Xerox Corporation's decline in photocopier sales. He succeeded and the lessons learned during that process form the basis for benchmarking today. Successful organisations were noticed to share most of the following features, which can still be a useful, if crude, set of indicators of the likelihood of benchmarking success.

- They have a fast flow of information between management and staff.
- They perform best when there is someone in the senior management team who understands the logistics of the organisation.
- They are aware that extra management levels cost time and money, as indeed does benchmarking and managing change.
- In successful organisations, change is not seen as a threat to individual or institutional competence.
- They regard all processes as having the potential to improve.
- They encourage a climate of continuous improvement.

Comparative benchmarking is often seen as a means to increase effectiveness, but it can increase efficiency as well. It can reduce correction costs by providing better training, better management and greater responsiveness. Consequently, professional disgruntlement can be reduced and productivity increased. Disenchantment, we are continually told, is a pre-eminent feature of life among teachers and school managers today and the cost to effectiveness should not be underestimated. Teachers sometimes report that managers are not responsive to their professional needs and managers in turn despair at their own inability to increase effectiveness and efficiency while fulfilling the school's mission in ever more difficult circumstances.

Comparative benchmarking can also reduce assessment costs, since appraisal, evaluation and change are automatic in the benchmarking organisation and therefore less management time is spent on major inspections than would otherwise be the case. For example, in schools and Further Education colleges, much effort is typically expended in the run-up to an Ofsted/Funding Council inspection. Often this effort is not aimed at improving output in terms of student learning, but at improving presentation and as such is wasteful. Benchmarking institutions have no need for such frantic exercise, since the cycle of evaluation and improvement is a naturally continuous and on-going one.

Finally, benchmarking can reduce the loss in income which results from failure. In schools and colleges, this could mean halting a decline in enrolment, improving staff planning or better relations with parents and the wider community.

Educational institutions frequently experience what could be called an 'inward spiral of decline'. Ineffectiveness may lead to poor examination results or poor discipline, for example, which in turn leads to declining enrolment, staff redundancy, scarcer resources and a consequent loss in effectiveness. Comparative benchmarking, as an alternative, seeks to provide an 'outward spiral of improvement', where ineffectiveness leads to self-examination and comparison with more successful organisations. This in turn leads to change, redesign, improvement, continuous assessment and greater effectiveness (Figure 2.1).

Comparative benchmarking encourages loyalty in customers, who perceive a learning institution committed to improvement. As a rule-of-thumb, for schools whose pupils are younger than the school-leaving age, the customer is the parent; for schools and colleges whose students are in post-compulsory education, the customer is the student. Notwithstanding this subtlety, the truism about loyalty still obtains. Today's students

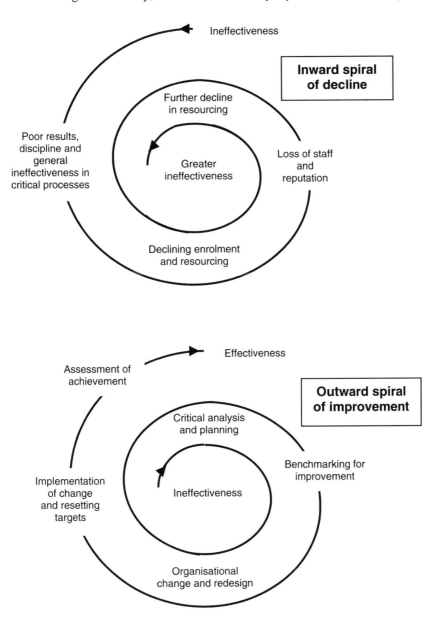

Figure 2.1 Spirals of decline and improvement.

are intuitively aware of the effect of quality assurance on educational outcomes and it would be a mistake to suppose that young people in schools or colleges are merely passive recipients of collective institutional wisdom. They are pro-active customers in education, as they are in the fashion, entertainment and music industries.

Benchmarking is a process that compares what is done internally ('what *we* do') with what competitor organisations do with similar processes ('what *they* do'). Simultaneously, it is a balance between analysing *what* is done, i.e. achieving an outcome, and *how* it is done, i.e. adapting a process. Together, these components alternate to make a comparative benchmarking spiral, which Figure 2.2 attempts to represent, echoing the outward spiral of improvement in Figure 2.1.

Benchmarking in schools and colleges is particularly apt today, with curriculum development and societal expectations changing so quickly. Schools and colleges need to be sensitive and responsive to these changes. They cannot afford to be inward looking, nor can they afford to rely solely on their institutional experience. Schools and colleges must gather what information they can, from wherever they can, in order to survive and thrive. Benchmarking is not a luxury; it is a necessity. (Figure 2.3 shows the steps involved.)

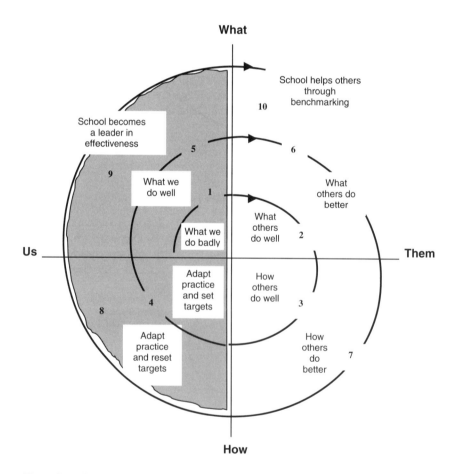

Figure 2.2 The benchmarking spiral.

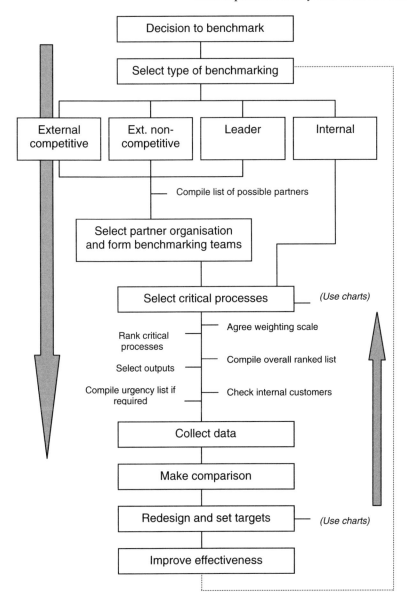

Figure 2.3 The process of benchmarking.

Choosing the critical processes

The decision to benchmark is easy. A more difficult task is choosing the processes to benchmark and the type of benchmarking. Improving some or all of an organisation's processes can make a real difference to overall effectiveness. However, some processes are 'critical' while others are merely 'functional' and it is important to distinguish between the two. Critical processes are ones which, if done badly, result in the organisation failing to achieve its primary purpose. For example, in a retail organisation like a high street supermarket where the primary purpose is to sell for profit, critical processes include cash flow management, pricing and stock control. In an educational institution, critical processes are more varied because the desired outcome – the primary purpose – is more vague (Figure 2.4).

Functional processes are ones which are undertaken merely to fulfil legal or statutory obligations. They are the processes that preserve institutional life, but do not serve the higher purpose for which the institution was established. Functional processes are not suitable for benchmarking, because they do not focus on improvement or what is a critical to success. Figure 2.5 gives a sample list of some functional processes for schools and colleges.

Deciding on critical processes may be, for some schools and colleges, simply a matter of having a meeting or a series of meetings at the appropriate managerial level, but in many educational institutions, where there is a multitude of independent working units within a complex organisation, a widespread sense of the overall institutional mission is often missing. In order to focus on critical processes in such a compartmentalised environment, it is often desirable to get participants to prioritise the processes they perceive as critical within their own particular areas. Some form of scoring or weighting may be used, so that priorities from different parts of the organisation may be drawn together in an overall list. Figure 2.6 shows one such weighting system.

Some critical processes: Pastoral	Some critical processes: Curriculum	Some critical processes: Administration and leadership
Staff consultation process	Staffing deployment	Policy-making process
Student and parent consultation	Timetabling: student liaison	Financial management
Discipline process	Timetabling: staff liaison	Distribution of funds
Careers guidance	Recruitment and redundancy	Promotion and appraisal
Personal and social guidance	Responding to change	Dissemination of information
Home–school liaison process	Quality control: teaching	Staff development
Complaints process	Quality control: learning	Industrial relations
External liaison process	Assessment of examinations	Ancillary services
Quality assurance of systems	Quality assurance of systems	Quality assurance of systems

Figure 2.4 Sample list of critical processes for a school or college.

Some functional processes
Health and safety at work requirements
Fair employment practice
Contractual obligations
Reporting truancy and illegal activities
Keeping records of attendance
Ofsted / FEFC inspection processes
Keeping abreast of requirements
Financial auditing
Keeping records of attainment

Figure 2.5 Sample list of functional processes for a school or college.

Type of critical process	Weight	
Directly and immediately affects teaching and learning	100	
Has indirect or delayed effect on teaching and learning	90	
Directly affects student performance	80	Most
Indirectly affects student performance	70	critical
Directly affects teacher performance	60	
Has indirect or delayed effect on teacher performance	50	
Affects efficiency or provision of resources with direct immediate effect on classroom activity	40	
Affects efficiency or provision of resources with indirect or delayed effect on classroom activity	30	Most functional
Administrative processes	20	
Functional processes	10	

Figure 2.6 A sample weighting system.

For every process that is identified as critical, an internal customer and an output should also be identified. An 'internal customer' is a member of staff who will buy into the new improved version of the process, if one emerges from the benchmarking process. If there is no internal customer for a critical process, then it is pointless to benchmark it. Internal customers must drive the changes resulting from benchmarking and as much consensus as possible should be achieved. Benchmarking should not be imposed by managerial diktat or by a remote team of apparatchiks.

'Critical outputs' are what result from these critical processes. By focusing on output, internal customers can identify how their critical processes contribute to the overall mission of the organisation. In addition, it saves the benchmarking process from being perceived as personal criticism and aspires to (at least) a partially quantitative comparison between organisations or parts of an organisation. Figure 2.7 shows typical outputs for some typical critical processes in schools and colleges. Most critical processes will have more than one output – sometimes many – and the benchmarker should aim to select a variety of both quantitative and qualitative measures for the purposes of comparison.

Benchmarking in this way – scoring individual processes in different areas of the organisation, selecting output and internal customers – focuses improvement on particularly critical areas. Of course, it is possible, in theory at least, to look at every process of an organisation and this would undoubtedly be the most rigorous approach. However, in the real world, where resources are finite and time so valuable, the extra expenditure is unlikely to make a commensurate difference to the result.

Prioritising the critical processes

Having gathered the most critical processes from each division of the organisation, the next step is to agree a list of the most urgent ones, without regard to managerial division, but with as much consensus and consistency as possible. Since any table of critical processes is drawn up from prioritised lists determined by the organisation's internal customers, it can be customised for each institution so that the most urgent problems are tackled first. Each organisation's 'urgency list' (Figure 2.8 shows a sample) will be different, depending on its circumstances and organisational maturity, but in all cases,

Critical processes	Some critical outputs
Staff consultation process	Staff morale and professional satisfaction
Student and parent consultation	Confidence and awareness
Discipline process	Exclusion and suspension rates
Careers guidance	Employment and progression rates
Personal and social guidance	Customer confidence and awareness
Home–school liaison process	Retention rates
Complaints process	Time in disputes and customer satisfaction
External liaison process	Community and business involvement
Staffing deployment	Staff and subject comparisons
Timetabling: student liaison	Customer satisfaction
Timetabling: staff liaison	Staff morale and professional satisfaction
Recruitment and redundancy	Staff turnover rates
Responding to change	Confidence
Quality control: teaching	Competence
Quality control: learning	Competence
Assessment of examinations	Comparison of examination results
Quality assurance of systems	Efficiency and effectiveness comparisons
Policy-making process	Professional satisfaction and awareness
Financial management	Per-capita and nature of expenditure
Distribution of funds	Per-capita and nature of expenditure
Promotion and appraisal	Staff morale and internal promotion rates
Dissemination of information	Awareness
Staff development	Attendance of staff at courses
Industrial relations	Time lost through disputes
Ancillary services	Resources used to support teaching

Figure 2.7 Critical processes and some critical outputs.

Urgent critical processes	Weight	Suggested outputs
Discipline process	90	Measurement of exclusion and suspension rates Measurement of student, teacher and parent satisfaction Measurement of student, teacher and parent awareness
Quality control of teaching	100	Measurement of attendance, punctuality, examination achievement, etc. Data from peer assessment and sharing experience Measurement of student and teacher self perception
Examination analysis	50	Analysis of results, subject-by-subject, in relation to national averages and Year 7 intake (SATs, etc.) Measurement of progression rates to employment, Further and Higher education Measurement of teacher and student satisfaction
Home school liaison	70	Measurement of retention and truancy rates Measurement of quantity and nature of complaints Measurement of parent and teacher satisfaction
Staff development	60	Measurement of attendance at professional development courses Measurement of time and resources spent on professional development Measurement of teacher satisfaction

Figure 2.8 A sample urgency list.

when the most urgent improvements are eventually made, other critical processes take their turn in the benchmarking queue. It should always be remembered that comparative benchmarking is a continuous process, not a fixed outcome.

Since the framework for scoring the relative importance of individual critical processes is so crucial, it is often a contentious and emotionally charged issue. In a school or college setting, it is likely to affect deputy heads, vice-principals and middle line managers in particular. A sensitive, almost empathetic, approach to benchmarking is likely to pay dividends in the long run, particularly if under-performance is due to ignorance rather than innate incompetence. For these very reasons, some organisations (at least initially) find it easier to employ external benchmarking consultants, rather than undertake it in-house.

For those organisations that choose to benchmark themselves, scoring the relative importance of different critical processes is very important. If weighting systems are used, they should be agreed among those members of staff who are initially most affected, remembering that it is more important to arrive at a general consensus than to construct some mathematically intricate system, and tweaking the weighting system is usually both possible and necessary.

While simple weighting is one method of prioritising processes, another method is to survey staff opinion using two complementary scorecards (Hutton and Zairi, 1994). One scorecard measures the 'strategic importance' of each process (Figure 2.9a); and the other measures the 'ease' with which staff think it can be benchmarked (Figure 2.9b) (Zairi, 1996). The scores for ease and importance are then plotted as a co-ordinate pair on a grid like the one shown on Figure 2.10. The scale on each axis can be drawn to accommodate the range of responses obtained from the staff scorecards.

Obviously, the ideal situation is to benchmark processes which are easily done and which are very important to the organisation's effectiveness – squares A on Figure 2.10. Other high scores come from critical processes which are easy to benchmark, but which are not very important – Squares B and D on Figure 2.10 – and from processes which are difficult to benchmark, but which are very important – Squares C and F on Figure 2.10. The situations become less favourable as one goes towards Squares K, where the processes are difficult to benchmark and are of little importance.

The order in which a team chooses to benchmark its critical processes depends on how desperate the school or college is for drastic improvement, although clearly, critical processes in Squares A should always be done first. If improvement is urgently sought, the team should move in the order ACFBEH . . . seeking out the processes that have high potential returns, irrespective of how difficult the processes may be to benchmark. If, on the other hand, it is more important to the organisation that *some* improvement be achieved, no matter how small the gain, then the team should follow the path ABDCEG . . ., seeking out the processes which are easy to benchmark, no matter what the return. The 'mixed' option is to follow the order ABCDEF . . ., balancing the risk and the potential gain.

Comparative benchmarking is a long and continuous process – a spiral of improvement – so it is important to have as many people on-board as possible. Whatever steps need to be taken to ensure that this is the case, should be taken. Self-criticism plays a vital role in benchmarking, so preliminary work sometimes has to be done to create a self-critical climate, as opposed to a climate of criticism. Self-criticism is part of professional reflection and one of the reasons why benchmarking is necessary in education is that change is driven by external factors. Benchmarking has to be a

SCORECARD **IMPORTANCE**	Name: Date:		
Critical process	**Max score**	**Actual score**	**Weight**	**Weighted score** Range 0–100

Critical process	Max score	Actual score	Weight	Weighted score
Staff consultation	10		5	
Student and parent consultation	10		7	
Discipline and rewards system	10		10	
Careers guidance	10		9	
Personal and social guidance	10		9	
Home–school liaison system	10		7	
Complaints procedure	10		7	
External liaison system	10		7	
Quality assurance	10		7	
Staffing deployment	10		10	
Timetabling: liaison with students	10		10	
Timetabling: liaison with staff	10		10	
Redundancy and recruitment of staff	10		7	
Staff induction	10		5	
Ability to respond to change	10		6	
Quality control: teaching	10		10	
Quality control: learning	10		10	
Prediction of attainment	10		3	
Policy-making process	10		3	
Financial management	10		4	
Internal distribution of funds	10		7	
Promotion and appraisal of staff	10		5	
Dissemination of information	10		5	
Staff development and training	10		6	
Industrial relations	10		6	
Ancillary services	10		2	

Figure 2.9a Sample staff scorecard: importance of critical processes.

continuous process since priorities change over time, as do the critical processes that most contribute to effectiveness. Consequently, reflection has to be both critical and continuous. It is better if staff take ownership of that reflection process and undertake participation in benchmarking with security and a sense of self-determination.

Mapping the critical processes

After a list of prioritised critical processes has been made, it is necessary to examine those urgent processes selected for benchmarking in greater detail, in order to understand the intricacies of what members of staff do to fulfil their functions within the organisation. What people do and what they say they do are not necessarily the same and it is often a good idea to represent the internal workings of each critical process on a

SCORECARD **EASE OF BENCHMARKING**	Name: Date:							
1 = very hard to benchmark 5 = very easy to benchmark			Please circle					
Critical process	**Actual score**						Weight	Weighted score
	Hard				Easy			Range 0–50
Staff consultation	1	2	3	4	5		5	
Student and parent consultation	1	2	3	4	5		7	
Discipline and rewards system	1	2	3	4	5		10	
Careers guidance	1	2	3	4	5		9	
Personal and social guidance	1	2	3	4	5		9	
Home–school liaison system	1	2	3	4	5		7	
Complaints procedure	1	2	3	4	5		7	
External liaison system	1	2	3	4	5		7	
Quality assurance	1	2	3	4	5		7	
Staffing deployment	1	2	3	4	5		10	
Timetabling: liaison with students	1	2	3	4	5		10	
Timetabling: liaison with staff	1	2	3	4	5		10	
Redundancy and recruitment of staff	1	2	3	4	5		7	
Staff induction	1	2	3	4	5		5	
Ability to respond to change	1	2	3	4	5		6	
Quality control: teaching	1	2	3	4	5		10	
Quality control: learning	1	2	3	4	5		10	
Prediction of attainment	1	2	3	4	5		3	
Policy-making process	1	2	3	4	5		3	
Financial management	1	2	3	4	5		4	
Internal distribution of funds	1	2	3	4	5		7	
Promotion and appraisal of staff	1	2	3	4	5		5	
Dissemination of information	1	2	3	4	5		5	
Staff development and training	1	2	3	4	5		6	
Industrial relations	1	2	3	4	5		6	
Ancillary services	1	2	3	4	5		2	

Figure 2.9b   Sample staff scorecard: ease with which critical processes can be benchmarked.

diagram. This is known as 'mapping' the critical processes and an example is set out on Figure 2.11.

Maps should be shown to participating staff and agreed with them as part of the benchmarking process – it reassures staff and helps to ensure that the critical process is fully understood and accurately represented.

Many successful schools and colleges have similar critical processes and follow a similar pattern. What makes one institution different from another is the way in which the different critical processes are internally structured and how they interact with

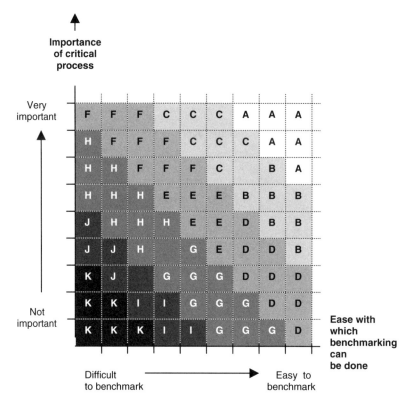

Figure 2.10 Grid for prioritising critical processes. (After Zairi, 1996.)

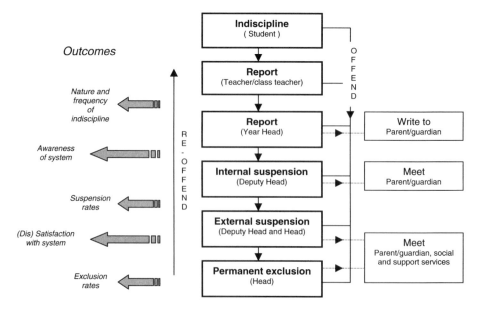

Figure 2.11 Internal map of a critical process: discipline.

one another. This is why successful benchmarking needs both a macroscopic and a microscopic view. The latter is got from understanding the detailed internal workings of the various critical processes and the former is got from putting the processes together so that they form a coherent representation of the organisational whole.

Systems programming

The interaction between processes and between the macroscopic and the microscopic complicates the process of benchmarking, but a number of techniques have been developed to expose the essentials. The most common involve the use of flow charts, tree diagrams, chain diagrams and matrices.

Flow charts

There are many types of flow chart, but the four that are easiest to use are: linear symbolic; two-dimensional symbolic; arrow; and herringbone. Figures 2.12a–d show one of each, using one school's critical process of discipline as an example.

The more quantitative the output, the easier the critical process is to benchmark. So critical processes with purely quantitative output, like funding, staffing and like-for-like examination results, are easier to benchmark than the likes of discipline, customer satisfaction and professional development.

Flow charts are designed to communicate sequential steps in an efficient way. The use of different symbols in both linear (Figure 2.12a) and two-dimensional symbolic (Figure 2.12b) flow charts represents different categories of sub-process and facilitates *post facto* analysis. Flow charts give a good overall view, with annotation, and one can see at a glance what type of sub-process, if any, dominates. Two-dimensional symbolic flow charts give a better idea of the process flow over time than the linear type, but with less annotation. Flow charts appear deceptively simple, but great care should be taken to represent all possible lines of flow, not just the obvious ones.

Arrow (Figure 2.12c) and herringbone (Figure 2.12d) flow charts are simpler than linear symbolic flow charts. They do not differentiate between the different types of sub-process, but can be used to represent complicated situations or where less detail is required. Arrow charts can point to unnecessary interactions between steps within or between critical processes – typically represented by an unnecessary arrow – but care should be taken to only represent the proven and significant relationships, otherwise the diagram becomes both unreliable and impossible to decipher. Herringbone charts illustrate processes or sub-processes that contribute to output and are typically represented by lines that join the main 'artery output line'. Lines that do not join the main artery do not contribute directly to output and should be examined carefully. Herringbone charts are simple to analyse, but unfortunately do not show any inter-dependency that might exist within the many processes and sub-processes.

Tree diagrams

Figure 2.13 shows a tree diagram, for the same disciplinary process. Tree diagrams are usually used to represent the interaction between component processes, with sub-processes represented by 'branch' lines.

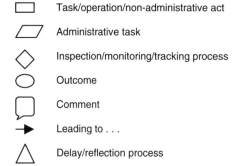

Task/operation/non-administrative act

Administrative task

Inspection/monitoring/tracking process

Outcome

Comment

Leading to . . .

Delay/reflection process

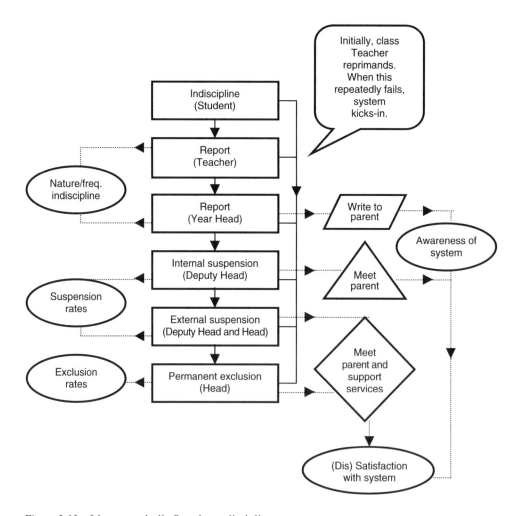

Figure 2.12a Linear symbolic flowchart: discipline.

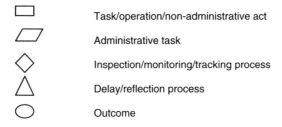

Task/operation/non-administrative act

Administrative task

Inspection/monitoring/tracking process

Delay/reflection process

Outcome

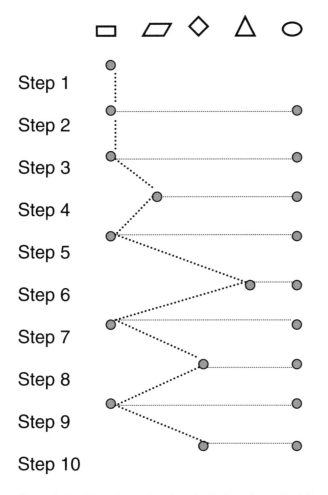

Figure 2.12b Two-dimensional symbolic flowchart: discipline.

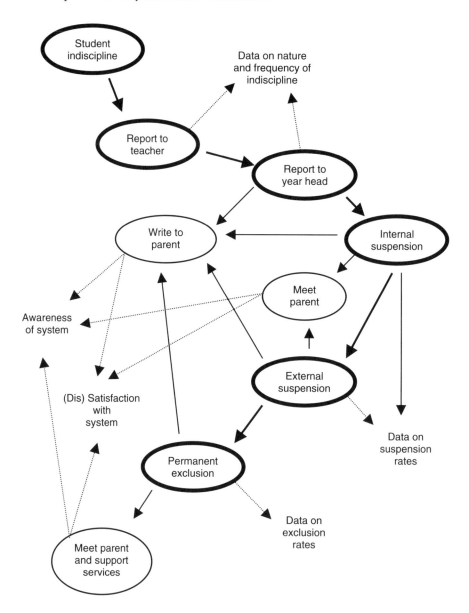

Figure 2.12c Arrow flowchart: discipline.

Chain diagrams

Figure 2.14 shows a linear chain diagram, though some chain diagrams can be circular. They are used to highlight the inter-dependency of sub-processes within a critical process and can illustrate how and why good teamwork should be put to use in a complicated organisation.

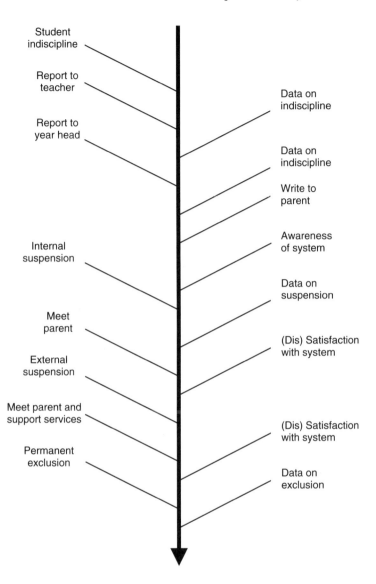

Figure 2.12d Herringbone flowchart: discipline.

Matrix diagrams

Figure 2.15 shows a matrix diagram which compares two schools and one college in terms of suspension rates, exclusion rates, complaints about discipline, parent visits and warning letters to parents. Matrix diagrams are usually only used during the final stages of benchmarking, to compare like critical processes in terms of their sub-processes, across institutions. The lower half of the diagram shows how each of the three organisations assessed their own target-setting, from 'historic' at the too easy end, to 'unlikely' at the too difficult end.

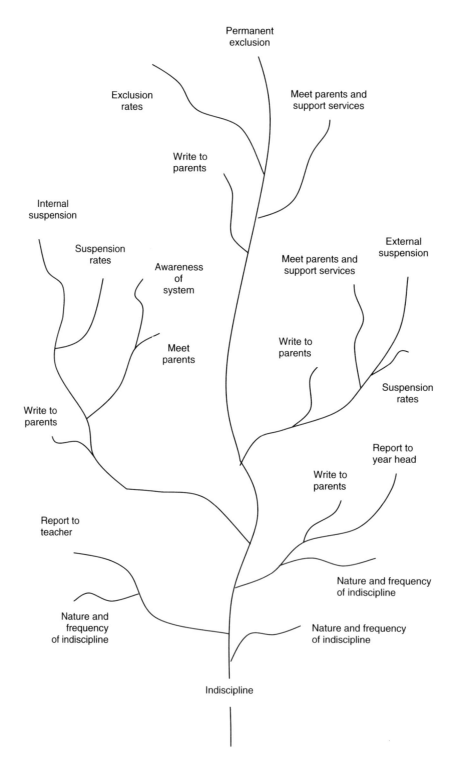

Figure 2.13 Tree diagram: discipline.

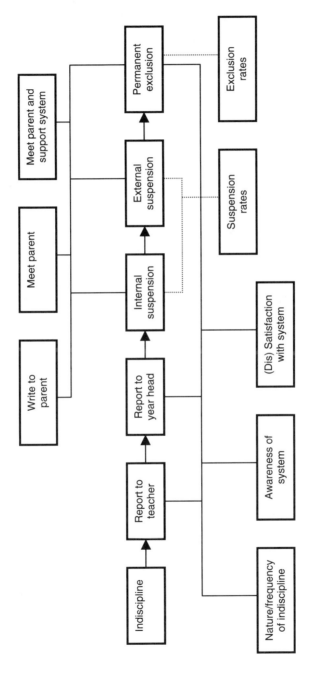

Figure 2.14 Chain diagram: discipline.

	Number of parent visits (%)	Suspension rates (%)	Exclusion rates (%)	Number of complaints (%)	Number of warning letters (%)
St. John's	13%	12%	2%	2%	17%
Star College	10%	7%	6%	2%	5%
Valley H.S.	23%	8%	0%	4%	15%

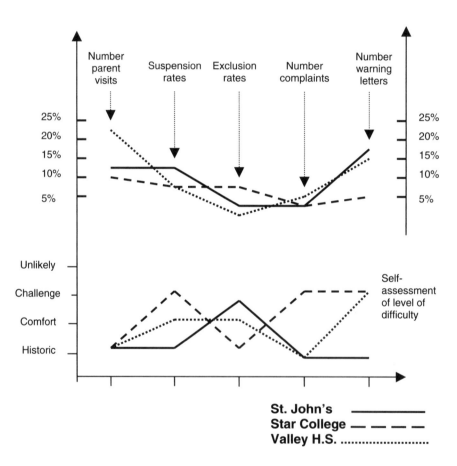

Figure 2.15 Part of a matrix diagram.

There is no hard and fast rule about which mapping technique should be used for which step in the benchmarking process, other than to say that they should be suited to the critical process involved. Diagrammatic representations of critical processes should always be checked with the personnel involved to ensure accuracy and encourage participation, and should be capable of being easily understood as part of the dissemination process that is a vital part of benchmarking.

Summary

- This chapter examined the rationale behind comparative benchmarking:
  - its necessity for survival;
  - the creation of an internal market;
  - its ability to compare processes across disparate organisations;
  - the fact of introducing tried and tested methods from elsewhere;
  - its ability to improve efficiency as well as effectiveness and promote customer loyalty.
- The difficult task of selecting critical (as opposed to functional) processes from among a multitude of organisational units was discussed.
- The notions of internal customers, weighting systems, ease and importance were used to construct a prioritisation grid, and systems programming for critical functions was described in terms of the various types of flow charts, tree diagrams, chain diagrams and matrix diagrams.

3 Internal and external non-competitive benchmarking

Forming a consortium

Forming a consortium is more than merely choosing a single non-competitive partner and establishing formal links with it. Best practice in comparative benchmarking is to establish links with several partners from different organisations or from within one organisation. In this way, different critical processes may be compared independently with different partners, widening the experience of those involved and speeding up the benchmarking process.

Partnerships

There are four broad categories of partnership.

- Partnerships between organisational units within a single school or college.
- Partnerships between organisations from a local educational network, such as a local education authority or a Further Education partnership.
- Partnerships with organisations in the same geographical area, not part of a local network, or not in the education sector.
- Partnerships with organisations (educational or non-educational) recognised as leaders in their field, irrespective of geographical location or sector, not covered by the first three categories. Such partnerships may even be established across international boundaries. For example, a school in the United Kingdom may set up a benchmarking partnership for effectiveness in foreign language teaching with a school in continental Europe teaching English.

The first two categories essentially concentrate on benchmarking within the 'home' organisation or network of organisations and this is often the most convenient starting point. Access to detailed information is likely to be relatively easy. The organisations (or parts of the organisation) are likely to be operating under similar circumstances and the exchange of data is likely to be relatively prompt. However, there are disadvantages.

First, component parts of an organisation or network tend to be competitive even though they are working in a cooperative environment and share the same overall objectives. Partner schools and colleges in a local education authority or within a more loosely defined educational consortium are outwardly cooperative, but latently competitive, and it would be a mistake to suppose that this reality does not impinge on the dynamics of comparative benchmarking. They often compete for resources from a central fund and to be perceived as the most effective organisation in the network can be advantageous. If it is the case that the spirit of competition has outstripped the spirit of cooperation within the organisation or network, then it is as well to benchmark with another institution outside the immediate geographical area or one operating in a different sector. Either way, the sensitivity required by those involved in the benchmarking process to the micropolitics of organisations such as schools and colleges, cannot be overstated. Political awareness – even astuteness – is a prerequisite for successful benchmarking.

The second major disadvantage to benchmarking within one organisation or network is familiarity. It is the enemy of radical change. Peer-group pressure from friends and colleagues is likely to result in less spectacular gains in efficiency and effectiveness than would otherwise have been the case. Figure 3.1 shows the steady, but unspectacular progress likely to be achieved within such an organisation or network. While it might appear in itself to be commendable, a comparison with Figure 3.2 shows how much short of the mark it actually falls.

Figure 3.2 is a 'step graph'. Each step represents a radical gain in effectiveness and such spectacular improvement in performance can only come about with radical thinking and an approach to benchmarking uninhibited by over-familiarity. Such progress is rarely achieved through internal benchmarking.

The third category – partnership with non-competitive organisations not part of a local network, but in the same geographical area – usually means a school forming a benchmarking partnership with a Further Education college, some other education-centred organisation (e.g. an Awarding Body or Examination Syndicate) or with organisations from outside the education sector. Such benchmarking partnerships can be very fruitful, offering as they do an opportunity to examine totally different ways of performing familiar tasks. The process can lead to genuine innovation and a spectacular step improvement in effectiveness. Experience has shown that the greatest step improvements come from benchmarking partnerships formed between schools or colleges and organisations from outside education. Very often, these for-profit organisations are well known to the school or college, through links such as those established by existing students on work experience or former students working full-time after they

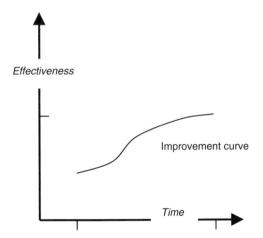

Figure 3.1 Benchmarking within an organisation.

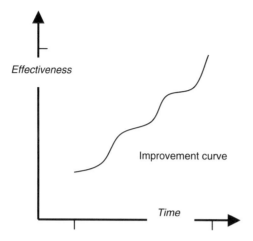

Figure 3.2 Benchmarking between organisations.

have left school or higher education. Alternatively, the commercial organisation may be a service provider or a supplier to the school or college; or links may already have been established by the careers staff. Schools and colleges should not be reluctant to develop existing relationships such as these for use in benchmarking partnerships, remembering that all parties to the consortium benefit from participation.

The fourth category – partnerships with organisations recognised as leaders in their field – is the optimal approach to benchmarking. Unfortunately, for most schools and colleges, it is also the least practical. Companies that are widely acknowledged to be leaders in particular critical processes tend to operate on a higher plane, due in part of course to the very success that comes from being so effective. Their use as benchmarking partners for schools and colleges is therefore limited, but the possibility should not be completely discounted. Many of the world's leading companies recognise the importance of recruitment and public relations, and may be willing to lend assistance (rather than participate) for that reason.

It is relatively easy to compile a list of assorted publicly-quoted companies that have outstanding reputations for effectiveness in particular critical areas: biotechnology companies for innovation; budget airlines for systems management; luxury car manufacturers for customer awareness; and leading fashion brands for marketing. If leading companies operate in the same geographical catchment area as an ambitious school or Further Education college, then they should be approached with a view to forming or informing a benchmarking consortium. Although the probability of a polite refusal is high, they just might offer to give initial guidance, especially if the approach appears to be a serious professional attempt at improvement. In addition, most leading companies have highly skilled employees and managers whose families have probably settled in the area and who want the option of high-quality education for their children. Failing that, there is always the possibility of an appeal to altruism, but it should be remembered that many top companies charge for their time and resources – a fact which should be checked at the outset, before any agreement to proceed is reached.

Compiling a shortlist

Irrespective of the type of consortium formed, a shortlist of potential partners needs to be compiled. Typically, such a list has between five and ten organisations on it. Each potential consortium partner should be investigated thoroughly, as far as possible without making official contact. When contact is eventually made, it will be a sign of professionalism and serious intent that such thorough research has been done. It will be seen as flattering rather than underhand. Comparative benchmarking is a symbiotic relationship. The school seeking benchmarking partners needs to create a good impression just as much as the organisation being selected – the partners chosen also have to choose!

Most organisations seeking to set up comparative benchmarking partnerships start by compiling information on potential partners and this can be obtained from among the following sources.

- Newspapers and relevant magazines. Back issues can be found in libraries and on the internet.
- Professional journals, which can be accessed in universities and specialist libraries.
- The internet. Often, the company being researched will have its own web-site, which will give basic information on policy, experience and structure. The information should of course be tempered by the knowledge that the web-site is designed to show the company in the best possible light. Beware the 'halo' effect.
- Personal contacts and former employees can be useful sources of information, though care should be taken not to encourage any breach of confidentiality. In addition, benchmarkers should beware of disgruntled former employees creating a 'horns' effect.
- Professional associations (such as the Learning and Skills Development Agency, the Local Government Association, the Secondary Heads Association, and so on) can sometimes be used to put potential benchmarking partners in contact with one another.
- Finally, there is no substitute for attending educational conferences, seminars and other networking events in order to make personal contact with benchmarking professionals from other schools and colleges.

Having compiled a shortlist of possible benchmarking partners and having investigated their strengths and their weaknesses, the next step is to reduce the number of possibilities using a variety of criteria.

Organisational size is one important selection criterion for shortlisting benchmarking partners. Large schools and colleges have economies of scale which make it very difficult for smaller institutions to copy their critical processes. This is not to say that benchmarking partners must be of similar size – it simply depends on what critical processes are being benchmarked. For example, benchmarking partners should be of broadly similar size when benchmarking critical processes such as per-capita staffing costs and administrative overheads. Size is less important if the critical process being benchmarked is disciplinary structure or examination results, say.

Other shortlisting criteria include: geographical location – a considerable number of meetings will need to be arranged, though much of the initial data collection and subsequent target-setting can be done independently; and compatibility and suitability – each school or college should be clear about what it wants from the partnership and consortium partners should be capable of developing good open working relationships as the process gets underway.

Generally, the more carefully the organisations are selected for the benchmarking partnership, the less chance there is that the process will have to be aborted later on.

The early stages of contact within a consortium

At this stage, a clear picture should have been formed by the initiating organisation of how the consortium will function and what critical processes are likely to be benchmarked. A letter should be sent to each selected partner outlining the purpose of the approach, why the organisation was chosen as a partner and the benefits of membership of the benchmarking consortium. A personal visit should be arranged by telephone, following receipt of the letter, allowing the partner plenty of time to make adequate preparation. They will want to create a good first impression too.

Considerable preparation should be given to this initial contact stage. It is fairly safe to assume that most schools and colleges are familiar with the general concept of comparative benchmarking, but if that is not the case, whatever time is necessary should be given in the first few meetings to outline its general practice, theory and benefit. The only useful partner is an informed one and many benchmarking partnerships have been abandoned at this early stage through lack of understanding.

Meetings should be friendly, but formal. An agreed agenda should be used, particularly for the first face-to-face visit and it is a good idea for the initiating organisation to suggest that another organisation host or chair the meeting. Simple manoeuvres like this get the partnership off to the right start, creating a shared sense of purpose and mutual trust. One word of warning: attempts to turn benchmarking meetings into therapy sessions about government funding or Ofsted inspections should be firmly resisted!

All meetings should be formally minuted, as it is frequently the case in comparative benchmarking that there are long gaps between meetings while data collection and analysis is taking place. It is also an unfortunate fact of life that the representative personnel involved in the benchmarking process can change over time. Well-documented meetings and a schedule of visits make it easier and less time-consuming for new personnel to join in and carry the process forward, when and if that becomes necessary.

The initial series of meetings should concentrate on finalising agreement of what each participating school or college most wants from the benchmarking process. Most of this will already have been done during the initial site visits, but it will be necessary to firm up expectations and more importantly, to document them. A brainstorming session is often a useful way of breaking the ice and getting everybody involved, though it needs to be carefully managed so that a range of both quantitative and qualitative output is selected.

Participating organisations should avoid the 'squirrel' approach to gathering data – hoarding unnecessary information for its own sake in the hope that one day, in some vague kind of way, it will be useful. Concentration should be on essentials, like how and why critical processes are undertaken in partnering organisations and mapping them in some agreed format.

After the initial series of meetings

At first, meetings should be fairly frequent and closely spaced. As the process unfolds, they will tend to concentrate less on tentative explorations and more on the core problems of 'how' and 'why'. As this happens, the importance of mapping critical processes increases, as does the need to support claims with hard data.

There are two ways in which the consortium can proceed at this stage. If there are more than two schools or colleges involved, they can form one-to-one relationships to examine only the critical processes that are of interest to them (Figure 3.3). Alternatively, all the organisations involved in the comparative benchmarking partnership can pool their critical processes for collective multiple comparison (Figure 3.4).

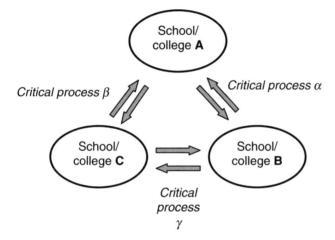

Figure 3.3 One-to-one approach within a consortium.

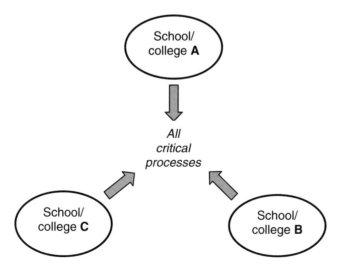

Figure 3.4 Collective approach within a consortium.

The advantage of the one-to-one approach is that it avoids involving organisations in comparing critical processes that are of no interest to them and speeds up the benchmarking process. The advantage of the latter collective approach is that it provides a broader basis for comparison and a more thorough benchmarking. Neither approach is necessarily more efficient or less time-consuming. It can take as much time working out what to avoid as being actively involved in everything, so it is largely a question of personal preference and the extent to which the partner organisations are mutually compatible.

Opting out of a benchmarking consortium

Sometimes proposals for a benchmarking partnership do not work out as intended. Partner organisations selected for participation, often through no fault of their own, turn out to be unsuitable. It may be the result of a clash of ethos or of purpose; it may be the result of unrealistic expectations; or it may be the case that one or more organisations simply cannot provide the necessary data. If this happens, it is better to abort the partnership earlier rather than later, though this can be a difficult thing to do if a friendly relationship has already been established. There is no easy way of doing it, but common courtesy dictates that it should be done face-to-face. Usually, all partners to the consortium realise that the partnership looks like being unproductive, in which case the break-up can be achieved without acrimony.

Benchmarking code of practice

It is often a good idea for benchmarking partners to agree some ground rules from the outset and these should form the basis of the partnership's code of practice. Experience has shown that the following principles are important.

- Discussions should not encourage a breach of professional confidentiality.
- Exchange of information should be on a like-for-like basis. It is not a true partnership if one school or college is offering far more sensitive information than it gets in return. Comparative benchmarking should be done in a spirit of openness.
- All information made available as part of the benchmarking process should be confined to that process and to those individuals and organisations involved. Certainly, information should never be divulged to any person or organisation outside the consortium without explicit permission. A successful partnership is one built on trust.
- The agreement to treat all information as confidential should extend beyond the life of the benchmarking partnership.
- Personnel involved in the benchmarking process from the various participating organisations should be of equal rank within their respective organisations. For example, they should all be deputy heads or vice-principals; or they should all be teachers or tutors with responsibility for benchmarking. An effort should be made to maintain this balance if and when others are co-opted.

- Responsibility should only be delegated to third parties with the agreement of all the organisations in the consortium.
- Personnel involved in the benchmarking process should realise the importance of adequate preparation for each meeting and at each stage. It is not helpful if the representatives from one school or college are less prepared than those from partnering institutions.
- Partnerships should strive to avoid giving the impression that they are involved in making cartel-like arrangements that will result in less choice for parents or students.
- Experience shows that it is better for all concerned if participating schools and colleges are up-front about what they will and will not disclose. It has been known for one organisation to give sensitive information freely in the expectation that something equally useful will be given in return, only to find that the partner refuses to divulge information of comparable sensitivity when the time comes.
- Personnel involved should have authority delegated to them by their respective managers before the benchmarking process gets much underway. It only encourages uncertainty and mistrust if representatives from an organisation have to continually refer back to management before participating fully in the exchange of information.
- Legal or other professional advice should be sought when and where appropriate. A party not involved in the benchmarking consortium can act as referee if need be and with the agreement of those involved.
- The benchmarking process should not be used to gain competitive advantage over partnering schools or colleges.
- All partnering organisations should be familiar with the consortium's code of practice and adhere to it.
- Successful benchmarking meetings should be professional, focused, punctual and firmly steered through the agreed agenda.
- Research tools, such as questionnaires and structured interviews, should be proforma across the consortium to ensure rigour and consistency.

Summary

- Chapter 3 considered the issue of forming a consortium for the purposes of comparative benchmarking against a non-competitor.
- Four broad categories of partnership were discussed:
    - internal to a school;
    - internal to a local network;
    - local but not educational;
    - partnerships, local or otherwise, with beacon organisations.

- The advantages and disadvantages of each were discussed and the need for step-change was illustrated.
- Shortlisting and selecting potential partners was dealt with briefly, and recommendations were made on such matters as:

- early stages of contact within a consortium;
- gathering and using benchmarking data;
- opting out of a partnership.

- Finally, a comprehensive code of practice for comparative benchmarking in education was presented.

4 Forming a benchmarking team within an organisation, collecting data and making an effectiveness comparison

Teambuilding

Just as partner organisations come together to form comparative benchmarking consortia, some staff must come together within each participating school or college to form benchmarking teams.

In any situation, teamwork should be based on mutual respect and a shared view of the objective. Comparative benchmarking teams additionally need to develop a shared understanding of what constitutes good benchmarking practice, since such an understanding is not widespread among teachers. This 'informative stage' in building a benchmarking team should be the priority initially.

The next stage in the team building process is to negotiate a role for each participating member, their commitment in terms of time and travel, and the allowances made for them by the head or principal as a result of their participation. This negotiation requires considerable management skill and credibility with staff, and is best done by a member of the senior management team. As mentioned already, authority needs to be delegated by the head or principal in order for the benchmarking team to function efficiently and a senior manager is best placed to take on the responsibility of leading it. If benchmarking expertise lies instead with middle managers, then clear guidelines on delegated authority need to be given. It should constitute almost complete freedom to engage with other organisations as part of the benchmarking process, as and when the leader sees fit. The team leader must take responsibility for the development of the benchmarking team and how well or badly it fulfils its objectives.

Some members of the benchmarking team will interface with consortium partners; others will disseminate practice internally or carry out data gathering and analysis. Whatever their roles, the team leader should encourage cooperation, commitment and open discussion among members. The team leader should remember the importance of not being perceived as elitist by the rest of the teaching staff, whose wider cooperation will be needed to implement improvement strategies after the 'comparison stage' of the benchmarking process has been completed. Additional staff should be able to join the benchmarking team at any stage, but the group interfacing with consortium partners should remain constant.

Team benchmarking is more time-consuming than the 'hero innovator' approach, but it does have benefits. It encourages wide subsequent acceptance of benchmarking among staff, reduces pressure on individuals, improves the quality of decision-making by drawing on collective expertise, increases motivation, reduces isolation and alienation, and improves communication within the school or college. As the benchmarking process moves from the comparison stage, through redesign, to the 'improvement stage', the benchmarking team can be disbanded or reconstituted as desired. Membership of the team is variable, not constant. It can and should be fluid and responsive to changing circumstances.

Senior management, of course, have obligations to resource the benchmarking team adequately, otherwise the implementation of change for improvement will be undermined. Ideally, benchmarking team members should be given reduced teaching loads for the period of their participation, particularly those who liaise with partner schools and colleges. Participation of staff should be voluntary, with some encouragement to those with particular expertise. Team members should have some familiarity with the critical processes being investigated and secretarial assistance should be provided. Participation will be strongest when it is based on the belief that the purpose is worthy of support and that will only be forthcoming when the process is perceived to be properly supported by senior management.

The benchmarking team should have a clear written statement of its purpose and timescale. Both should be realistic and achievable. It is often a good idea to concentrate initially on some well-defined short-term (one year) goals, otherwise the benchmarking budget may be commandeered to cope with more pressing problems. It should also be made clear to teaching staff how the benchmarking process fits into the greater scheme of things and the likely benefits accruing to the institution and to individuals.

Teams should be realistic in marrying the purpose and the timescale. Each team member should understand what is required and where their effort fits into the overall comparative benchmarking process. It is the team leader's job to match individual effort with the overall team objective and to see that reasonable resources are fairly allocated. In this respect, time management is likely to be more crucial than financial acumen.

Leaders should beware of relying too much on established practice at the expense of more efficient ways of operating. Major non-sequential tasks should be sub-divided and as far as possible, undertaken simultaneously, to save time. They should be drawn together later, in keeping with the overall planning strategy.

Although certain tasks should be sub-divided, the benchmarking team should not. Splinter groups detract from team spirit and blur the sense of purpose. They also make the task of review and planning more difficult and lengthier. For these reasons, benchmarking teams should be kept to a size commensurate with need, and the temptation to co-opt every friendly teacher should be resisted. When the initial benchmarking process has been completed, the benchmarking team may form the nucleus of a Quality Management Team within the school or college (see Chapter 7). A solid foundation will be required in that event so that there is continuity and expertise available for monitoring effectiveness and creating an 'organisational memory'.

Collecting benchmarking data

Once the critical processes to be benchmarked have been chosen, a system for gathering data should be installed. As has already been stated, each critical process selected for benchmarking should be mapped (see Figure 2.11) and checked with the personnel concerned to ensure accuracy, consistency and encourage confidence in the benchmarking process. Mapping forms the initial part of data collection and 'systems programming' represents the link between mapping individual critical processes and how these critical processes fit together in the overall structure of the organisation.

Most data comes from the output of the individual critical processes and can be hard, like exclusion rates, examination results, contact and pupil:teacher ratios; or soft, like staff morale, parental satisfaction, student awareness and reputation in the community. The benchmarking process should attempt some measure of balance between the two.

In attempting a balance between the hard quantitative and the softer qualitative data, it is vital that there is a consistency of approach across the different critical processes. Otherwise, comparisons within or between institutions are meaningless. The problem of consistency is not confined to soft output. Even hard quantitative data can be measured in different ways and those involved in the benchmarking process must be constantly alert to the inherent dangers. For example, something as straightforward as financial resourcing can be open to different interpretations. One institution might include income raised by fund-raising, while another might count only income from the local education authority through age-weighted pupil units.

The issue of consistency is one that particularly affects comparative benchmarking between schools and Further Education colleges, where typically a larger proportion of staff is part-time and hours of operation are more flexible. Further Education colleges also work in a different market and under different financial constraints.

The problems of consistency with softer output is more obvious, but no less difficult to resolve for that. Great care must be taken to ensure that outputs like satisfaction, awareness, morale and confidence are all measured in the same way across the consortium or within institutions. This requires some measure of coordination within and between benchmarking teams, but it is largely just a matter of having regular standardisation meetings.

The mechanisms of planning and data collection varies depending on which of the four types of benchmarking is used, but the underlying principle is always that like should be compared with like, as simply as possible, using a variety of different outputs to measure each critical process.

Data collection from external competitive benchmarking

Obviously, the need to ensure consistency across competing institutions is greater in the case of external benchmarking than in the case of internal benchmarking. Different schools and colleges have different ways of measuring similar outcomes and particular care needs to be taken when a secondary school and a Further Education college partner each other for benchmarking, or when a more effective institution is being shadowed by another.

Generally, it is a mistake to use information contained in promotional literature for benchmarking purposes and the temptation to do so should be resisted. Of course, mapping individual critical processes will help to standardise activities across partnering institutions, but this does not obviate the need to get background information – even for hard outcomes.

Collecting initial data on competitor institutions can require a large amount of detective work, since there is no partnership consortium and no agreement yet to cooperate. Background information may be gleaned from Ofsted or FEFC reports, examination returns, socio-economic statistics, local authorities, government publications and so on. Where possible, background information should be obtained over a number of years to help establish trends and support forecasts. Useful secondary sources of information on schools and colleges may be obtained from educational journals, newspaper cuttings, advertisements and web-based sites.

Data collection from external non-competitive benchmarking

The main feature of non-competitive benchmarking is that it is a partnership rather than a shadowing exercise. Therefore, personal contact is the norm rather than the aspiration and agreement is usually reached fairly quickly on a full and frank exchange of information. Unlike external competitive benchmarking, there is little inclination to use promotional literature and background information is usually exchanged as a matter of course. However, it should still be borne in mind that there might be differences in how the partnering schools or colleges measure their respective outputs. If this is the case, it is better to establish the facts at the beginning of the benchmarking process, before inferences have been drawn.

Since non-competitive benchmarking is the most easily accessible type of benchmarking for educational institutions, the process of setting up a consortium in an educational setting has been dealt with in some detail already. However, it is worth repeating that any comparative benchmarking between partners requires a high degree of planning and courtesy between participating personnel. Unprepared or unscheduled visits to partnering institutions should be avoided at all costs.

In certain circumstances, external non-competitive benchmarking may not involve direct contact with a partnering institution at all. For example, a school or college may decide to gather information from non-competitors by questionnaire or by interview. While this approach is undoubtedly very efficient, it does not constitute an exchange of information and there is little or no quality control. Additionally, it is frequently perceived as irksome by institutions to be asked to give generously of time and information, but to get nothing in return – a fact which explains the usually low returns for postal survey questionnaires.

Where the partner organisation to a school or college is from outside the education sector, benchmarkers need to be more creative than would otherwise be the case. They must be constantly on the lookout for ways in which to graft exemplary practice from outside education onto those extant within their schools or colleges.

Data collection from internal benchmarking

Gathering data from internal benchmarking is usually even less of a problem than from external non-competitive benchmarking, since all the personnel involved belong to the same school or college. However, commonsense and the usual warnings about consistency and standardisation still apply. Even in a single school or college, not all teachers or lecturers measure the outputs of their critical processes in the same way or using the same baseline. There can be as much variation within organisations as between them. For example, when comparing examination results, it might be necessary to gauge the breath of intake for each subject.

Difficult though it may be, it is important that benchmarkers divorce what they think they know about their colleagues' work from what they actually know. Since the subjects of the benchmarking process are colleagues who have to be convinced of its benefits and involved subsequently in the cycle of self-criticism and improvement, it is doubly important that benchmarkers strive to be objective and on their guard for 'halo and horns' effects. Not every output from a teacher perceived as effective is necessarily good; and the converse is true for those members of staff perceived to be weak. Sometimes quality is assumed to be present in a process or an output when it is not; and sometimes it is assumed to be absent when it is not.

Data collection from leader benchmarking

Leader benchmarking is a comparison with a known market leader with a reputation for outstanding practice. As a result, information is usually widely available from professional journals and the like. In any event, market leaders in an education setting are usually very happy to share their experiences and may even have a member of staff specifically designated to deal with inquiries from other schools or colleges.

Making an effectiveness comparison

Having selected partners, formed a benchmarking consortium, selected critical processes and formed a benchmarking team within each participating school or college, the next step is to make comparisons. This is the crux of benchmarking – investigating, by means of comparison, how and why another organisation can achieve greater effectiveness while carrying out similar critical processes. This 'performance gap' is what benchmarking hopes to close. Of course, analysing the performance gap and closing it are two different matters. Even while the benchmarking process is going on, the organisation with superior performance is probably forging ahead in terms of effectiveness, and consequently, the gap may be widening. Benchmarking organisations do not stand still. They continually strive to improve. Therefore, the 'inferior' organisation must aim for a steeper learning curve in order to close the gap (Figure 4.1).

Benchmarkers need to be ambitious just to keep up. Good benchmarking needs *current* data to be effective and this is one of the reasons why it is desirable to form consortia – historical data, by its very nature, is already out of date.

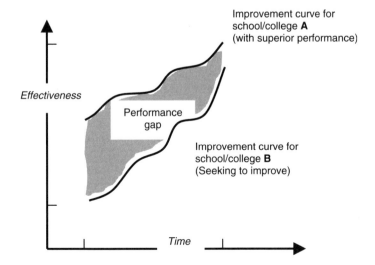

Figure 4.1 Closing the performance gap.

Benchmarking partners carry out their analyses of the performance gap (the 'process-to-process analysis') using a variety of tools. Sometimes it is enough to compare flow charts and see how critical processes differ. On other occasions, it is necessary to make comparisons using trend graphs, bar charts or scatter diagrams. There are as many ways of representing the comparison as there are critical processes. The only selection criterion is that of suitability – choosing a method of representation which can explain simply and quickly the essential differences between how the critical processes are made to function in the different schools and colleges. It is a good idea sometimes to illustrate the performance gap using more than one representation, particularly if the critical processes differ in a number of respects. One way or the other, the watchwords should be simplicity and self-discipline. Try to avoid statistical virtuosity which might flatteringly create the impression that benchmarking is one of the highest forms of human endeavour, but which is completely incomprehensible to staff.

An alternative way of proceeding is to list the factors which individual partners consider make for *ineffectiveness* in their own schools and colleges: lack of leadership; lack of managerial vision; poor communications; dysfunctional staff relationships; ineffective teaching, and so on (Figure 4.2). Rather than making a list of effectiveness determinants (as in Figure 5.2, p. 48) and seeking them out in benchmarking partnerships with the view to replicating them, this alternative way of proceeding is to seek out ineffectiveness determinants with a view to avoiding them.

This is what might be called 'negative benchmarking' (Figure 4.3). Instead of a performance gap between two schools or colleges which the inferior organisation seeks to close, there is a gap which the *superior* organisation seeks to widen, and ideally, these two 'disimprovement curves' should end up mutually perpendicular.

As has already been mentioned, benchmarking throws up both hard and soft measures of performance. Benchmarking should aim for a mixture of the two, but there will be a natural tendency to favour the quantitative, when such is available. This is understandable, since numerical measures are easier to compare, but it should not be assumed that soft qualitative measures of effectiveness are any less valuable. What is important is that like should always be compared with like – quantitative with quantitative and qualitative with qualitative – so that any process-to-process comparison is consistent and objective. Particular care should be taken when measuring things like attitude, satisfaction ratings and staff morale.

Benchmarking does not aspire to measure effectiveness against some rigidly defined mathematical yardstick. Rather it is a comparison, using the *same* yardstick, across two or more organisational units performing the same critical process. The yardstick itself is not important *per se*. What is important is that it is applied consistently. The same thing should be measured in both organisations, so that factors affecting effectiveness and efficiency which lie outside the control of the organisation, do not affect the validity of the benchmarking process.

Process-to-process analysis (i.e. analysing comparative performance) most frequently uses diagrams of one sort or another, which is why they were considered in such detail in the previous chapters. Previous benchmarking experience has shown that the most effective practices have fewer external influences, so benchmarkers must be careful to represent all possible external influences on any flow chart or diagram. The relative importance of these external influences as determinants need not be known precisely; what is important is that their presence is signposted.

Having analysed the performance gap for each critical process, the next step is to

CHARACTERISTIC	EFFECTIVENESS	INEFFECTIVENESS
LEADERSHIP	Firm and purposeful Supportive of staff and students Participative approach Instructional leadership Effective staff monitoring Encouraging positive climate	Vague and variable Isolated from staff and students Dictatorial. Disenfranchisement Absence of vision Casual staff monitoring Climate of obligation
TEACHING	Firm and purposeful teaching Structured lessons Flexible and efficient	Aimless and ad hoc approach Confusing lessons Inefficient, unresponsive and repetitive
LEARNING	Maximisation of class time Emphasis on achievement Pleasant environment Good organisation and structure	Teaching time lost Emphasis on getting course covered Disorganised environment, not conducive to teaching/learning
GOALS	Shared sense of vision Unity of purpose Sense of collegiality Spirit of co-operation	No vision or that of one manager Everyone acting in isolation Individualism Spirit of internal competition
DISCIPLINE	Firm, fair and transparent Orderly environment Responsive and sensitive Students held in high esteem Students given responsibility Reinforcing good behaviour	Strict. Emphasis on punishment Disorganised, at times chaotic Not geared to needs of learner Teacher centred, students regarded as passive recipients, not active participants in learning Relies on threat of punishment
EXPECTATION	High expectations of students High expectations of staff Challenging atmosphere Students take responsibility	Low expectations of students and staff Atmosphere of minimising work and 'getting by' Students not trusted to take responsibility
MONITORING & TRACKING	Regular evaluation of performance Effective tracking of progress Monitoring progress everywhere	Sole reliance on external inspection Absence of administrative systems for student progress Sporadic monitoring based on convenience
STAFF DEVELOPMENT	Careful selection of staff Careful induction of staff Spirit of institutional learning Co-ordinated approach	Haphazard recruitment Absence of induction programmes Institutional inertia Professional development left to individual teachers
PARENTAL INVOLVEMENT	Active home–school partnership Good communications	No parental participation No sense of partnership or serving a community Poor communications

Figure 4.2 Factors influencing effectiveness and ineffectiveness.

prepare targets for new, improved, more effective processes, so that the gap can be narrowed. While these are being prepared, the results of the benchmarking process should be disseminated within each individual school or college. Senior management and staff will need time to digest all the resource implications of the recommendations. It is often the case that the performance gap analysis reveals surplus elements in some

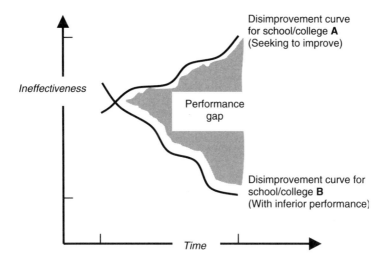

Figure 4.3 Negative benchmarking.

critical processes and these usually have serious implications for staffing, so the integrity of the benchmarking process must be beyond reproach. The benchmarking team should be fairly certain that any transplanted process is indeed transferable, i.e. that a more effective process adopted by another school will not fail in its new environment because it's very effectiveness was due to some unique set of circumstances that obtained there.

The benchmarking team should only recommend those process improvements that lead to step-change, as these are the ones most likely to achieve significant progress on that steep learning curve. Benchmarkers have to be both convinced and convincing. If there is to be pain, then it should be for an appreciable gain. Internal customers have to buy the product too, because the next stage is implementation.

Summary

- This chapter discussed forming teams within individual organisations party to a benchmarking consortium.
- The critical role played by senior managers and the need for credibility among non-participating staff were considered in some detail.
- Data collection and the issues of consistency and currency were shown to vary with the type of benchmarking being employed.
- The concepts of performance gap, negative benchmarking and the necessity for improving organisations to follow a steep improvement curve were also explained.

5 Redesign and targeting for improvement

Target-setting is a necessary part of benchmarking because it is only through ambitious target-setting can step-change be achieved (see Figure 4.1). However, target-setting in educational institutions differs in many respects from target-setting in the commercial sector.

- The nature of the stakeholders.
- The paradigm against which schools and colleges operate.
- The way effectiveness is defined for schools and colleges.
- The way effectiveness is achieved in schools and colleges.
- The way effectiveness is measured and the complicated nature of assessment in schools and colleges.
- The way extraneous factors are dealt with as part of the effectiveness inspection system.

The stakeholders

A simplified one-to-one correspondence can be made between the stakeholding interests in education and those in business, as reference to Figure 5.1 shows.

The similarities are striking and even extend beyond these seven categories. Membership of any one category, in either sector, is not exclusive. Teachers can be parents or

Business stakeholders	Education stakeholders
Customer Workforce Managers Directors Shareholders	Parents/students Teachers Heads, principals, managers Governors Government (on behalf of society)
Legal accountability to shareholders via Board of Directors	Legal accountability to government via Board of Governors
Moral accountability to customers and workforce	Moral accountability to parents, students and teachers

Figure 5.1 Comparison between business and education stakeholders.

governors; and workers can be customers, directors or shareholders. However, while each type of organisation aspires to measure its effectiveness and to improve upon it, there are subtle differences.

According to the Schools Standards and Framework Act (1998) and assorted DfEE guidance circulars, the Board of Governors is responsible for determining the aims of the school and with the head, how the school should go about improvement. The government (DfEE/Ofsted) sets the standards that schools are expected to attain, determines the content of the National Curriculum and decides on methods of assessment and testing. It provides targets for schools, which are linked to national targets for achievement at the four key stages and post-sixteen, and evaluates schools, teachers, heads and governing bodies against these criteria.

Therefore, in schools and colleges, different stakeholders are responsible for measuring effectiveness and for improvement. Measurement of effectiveness is the responsibility of government, while improvement is the responsibility of managers, on behalf of governing bodies. In commercial organisations, on the other hand, both measurement of effectiveness and improvement are the responsibilities of management, on behalf of boards of directors. There is no functional separation of effectiveness and improvement.

Paradigm and culture

In terms of paradigm, organisations in the education and business sectors differ in three main respects: shareholder value; customer obligation; and staff involvement.

In the business sector, effectiveness is judged powerfully by shareholder value, realising it and releasing it, even to the point of self-destruction. Shareholder value is king and that value is largely a measure of the organisation's potential for improvement, as perceived by the market. In schools and colleges, effectiveness is judged solely on historical performance. The greater the potential for improvement, the more trouble the school is in! Schools and colleges operate in a paradigm where historical performance is king.

The education paradigm is different too with regard to the set of obligations under which it operates. Under the Education Act (1998), schools are obliged to consult their customers (parents), who have statutory representation on governing bodies, but have no role in target-setting, so there appears to be an inherent assumption that governors and managers have the ability to know (or find out) what parents want as they undertake target-setting and improvement. The opposite is the case for organisations operating against a business paradigm. They have no statutory obligation to involve customers, although customers nevertheless lead the target-setting and improvement processes through customer relations focus groups and information gathered from loyalty cards and the like.

In the new 'post-Fordist' economy (Drucker, 1993), a workforce is now more valuable to an organisation for its adaptability and potential to contribute to improvement, than for its job-skills or expertise. Consequently, and increasingly, there is a culture of participation, partnership and responsibility in the for-profit sector. In education, on the other hand, teachers are valued more for their job-skills and generally have only a very loose relationship with policy-makers. The culture is one of delegation, obligation and response, with a lesser sense of partnership.

How effectiveness is defined

Defining effectiveness in business organisations is relatively easy. It is to increase share-holder value, or more accurately, to be effective in ways that increase shareholder value. Institutional aims are self-evident, whether tempered or not by environmental, ethical or historical considerations, and are articulated by the Board of Directors. Business is left to its own devices and its collective – the market – is deemed to know best. The state is content that any accruing benefit to the many is left to trickle down from the few.

Unfortunately, effectiveness and organisational aims are not so easily defined in schools and colleges. Is it the aim to develop the person as an individual, or the person as a member of society? Should schools train young people to meet the needs of the state, as determined by the state, or develop the inner person? Only occasionally, do these philosophical issues gain widespread prominence (for example, Callaghan's Ruskin College speech, 1976). For the most part, educational institutions struggle to achieve effectiveness against aims externally determined and internally articulated.

In any case, the manner in which Ofsted carries out its inspections has largely supplanted such philosophical considerations. Judging schools according to their league table performance presupposes that that is what is important. This may be a narrow, functionalist, view of achievement, but it is the one prevalent among those who judge the extent to which individual schools are effective. So, while governors and managers may or may not be aware of the various conflicting philosophical perspectives, the practical agenda has already largely been decided by the selection of criteria against which success is measured. Schools and colleges are not left to their own devices, like commercial organisations, and the education collective does not 'know best'. Trickle-down education, where quality for the few may eventually becomes equality for the many, is apparently deemed too risky a prospect to be left without state guidance.

How effectiveness is achieved

However effectiveness for schools and colleges is defined, research has, over the last two or three decades, distilled the factors which have improved it, so that a table can now be compiled of factors which are known to increase school effectiveness (Figure 5.2). These factors, which make for effective schools, act as a lower limit to the freedom of managers and teachers to act. Below this limit lies ineffectiveness and incompetence.

The upper limit is set by the narrow measurement criteria used by government inspection. Above the upper limit, achievement is not recognised. In fact, teaching above that level could be regarded as inefficient and unfocused, in that it expends unnecessary effort seeking unrecognised achievement (Figure 5.3).

These two limits act as boundaries to professional action and to what can reasonably be achieved or expected from benchmarking in education. No such boundary exists in the business sector. There is a corresponding lower limit of competence, of course, beneath which failure becomes apparent, but there is no upper limit set by measurement criteria. Consequently, managers are not as curtailed professionally in their freedom to act.

CHARACTERISTIC	DETAILS	BIBLIOGRAPHIC REFERENCES
LEADERSHIP	Firm and purposeful Supportive of staff and students Participative approach Instructional leadership Effective staff monitoring Encouraging positive climate	Mortimore *et al.*, 1988. Hopkins, Ainscow and West, 1994 Sammons, Thomas and Mortimore 1997. Hopkins, Ainscow and West, 1994 Mortimore *et al.*, 1988. Rutter *et al.*, 1979 Louis and Miles, 1990. Levine and Lezotte, 1990 Mortimore *et al.*, 1988 Mortimore *et al.*, 1988. Hopkins, Ainscow and West, 1994. Stoll and Fink, 1994
TEACHING	Firm and purposeful teaching Structured lessons Flexible and efficient	Rutter *et al.*, 1979. Good and Brophy, 1986 Mortimore *et al.*, 1988. Rutter *et al.*, 1979. Scheerens, 1992 Scheerens, 1992
LEARNING	Maximisation of class time Emphasis on achievement Pleasant environment Good organisation/structure	Rutter *et al.*, 1979. Alexander, 1997. Bennett, 1992 Sammons, Hillman and Mortimore, 1995 Creemers, 1994. Sammons, Hillman and Mortimore, 1995 Mortimore *et al.*, 1988. Rutter *et al.*, 1979. Scheerens, 1992
GOALS	Shared sense of vision Unity of purpose Sense of collegiality Spirit of cooperation	Louis and Miles, 1990. Sammons, Hillman and Mortimore, 1995 Levine and Lezotte, 1990. Sammons, Hillman and Mortimore, 1995 Fullan, 1991. Hopkins, Ainscow and West, 1994. Levine and Lezotte, 1990. Levine and Lezotte, 1990. Sammons, Hillman and Mortimore, 1995
DISCIPLINE	Firm, fair and transparent Orderly environment Responsive and sensitive Students held in high esteem Students given responsibility Reinforcing good behaviour	Rutter *et al.*, 1979. Sammons, Hillman and Mortimore, 1995 Lezotte, 1989. Sammons, Hillman and Mortimore, 1995 Mortimore *et al.*, 1988. Rutter *et al.*, 1979 Levine and Lezotte, 1990. Sammons, Hillman and Mortimore, 1995 Levine and Lezotte, 1990. Sammons, Hillman and Mortimore, 1995 Mortimore *et al.*, 1988. Rutter *et al.*, 1979
EXPECTATION	High expectations of students High expectations of staff Challenging atmosphere Students have responsibilities	Edmonds, 1981. Teddlie and Stringfield, 1993 Reynolds *et al.*, 1994. Sammons, Hillman and Mortimore, 1995 Mortimore *et al.*, 1988 Reynolds and Murgatroyd, 1977. Mortimore *et al.*, 1988
MONITORING AND TRACKING	Regular evaluation of performance Effective tracking of progress Monitoring progress everywhere	Hopkins, Ainscow and West, 1994 Mortimore *et al.*, 1988. Sammons, Hillman and Mortimore, 1995 Sammons *et al.*, 1995. Levine and Lezotte, 1990
STAFF DEVELOPMENT	Careful selection of staff Careful induction of staff Spirit of institutional learning Coordinated approach	Stringfield and Teddlie, 1987. Bridges, 1992 Mortimore *et al.*, 1988. Levine and Lezotte, 1990 Sammons, Hillman and Mortimore, 1995 Mortimore *et al.*, 1988. Levine and Lezotte, 1990
PARENTAL INVOLVEMENT	Active home–school partnership Good communications	Mortimore *et al.*, 1988. Levine and Lezotte, 1990 Mortimore *et al.*, 1988. Levine and Lezotte, 1990

Figure 5.2 Factors influencing school/college effectiveness.

How effectiveness is measured

Targets are set for schools by the DfEE at both national and local level, some of which are mandatory and some of which are optional. The Qualification and Curriculum Authority (QCA) and Ofsted support this target-setting process by providing information for local and national comparisons. Secondary schools have mandatory targets to reach at Key Stage 3 in the core subjects and in GCSE grades at Key Stage 4. Schools are also expected to choose a comparator, such as the percentage of pupils eligible for free school meals, so that a contextualised comparison can be made with other schools.

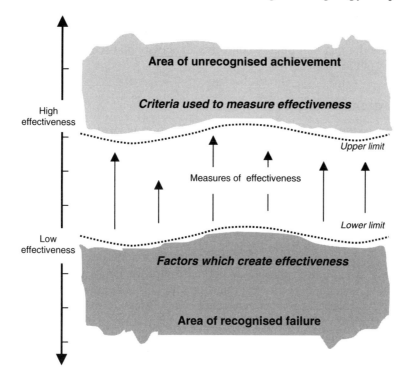

Figure 5.3 Limits to professional action.

There is no comparable target-setting in business organisations, except insofar as the market values a company by comparing its performance against others in the same sector. Managers who do comparatively well in an underperforming sector are highly regarded.

For both education and business sectors, target-setting is dependent on the quality of the information available. Fortunately, even in education, this can be of a very high quality and likely to get even better over time as more and better school and college inspections are carried out. Society is moving towards a state of near-perfect knowledge. Information is gathered more quickly, it is disseminated more efficiently and it is less precious in that it is more widely available and to a less expert audience. It is reasonable to assume therefore, that target-setting will in all aspects of society become more realistic and stakeholders better informed.

Quality assurance and quality control are both used extensively in the business sector to measure effectiveness. 'Quality assurance' is the determination, by inspection, of standards and methods (Murgatroyd and Morgan, 1993). It is a measure of the extent to which practice meets certain standards and it therefore concentrates on process. 'Quality control', on the other hand, is the inspection of an output after a process has been completed. It is carried out regardless of input and concentrates, not on process, but on determining whether the output is acceptable or not. In business, the emphasis shifts from one to the other, depending on the nature of the company. Industrial production companies tend towards quality control and service sector businesses tend towards quality assurance. Given the nature of each, it might be expected that assessment of effectiveness in education would incline towards the latter. Not so! The Ofsted inspection process concentrates more on quality control than on quality assurance, despite the fact that quality control is an activity that schools and colleges could easily carry out for themselves.

Dealing with extraneous factors

The term benchmarking, as used by the education inspection agencies, is norm-based. It constructs a median performance for schools operating in similar circumstances so that, by definition, there are some in the uppermost percentiles and some in the lowest (Figure 5.4). Effectiveness is then measured against this distribution. In other words, performance is benchmarked against *all* schools, rather than against the *best* schools. This is not benchmarking as the term is used in business, or in this book. For the DfEE (including the QCA and Ofsted), benchmarking focuses on results, rather than on processes. It measures how well a school has performed under a certain set of socio-economic circumstances, rather than why and how other schools operating in similar circumstances are doing better. Success is defined simply as being greater than the median and failure as being in the lowest quartile, say. This normative benchmarking does not facilitate comparison between schools in terms of their processes. It encourages isolationism, rather than cooperation. In fact, it acts as a disincentive, since effective schools are only judged successful because others are judged failures; an effective school helping a less effective one guarantees only to threaten its own performance assessment! It is ironic that, in the competitive world of business, benchmarking encourages cooperation, whereas in the cooperative world of education, it encourages hostility.

To sustain this system of normative benchmarking, extraneous factors have to be taken into account, although the extent to which a child's progress is determined by such factors is not yet known. Ofsted provides schools with Performance and Assessment

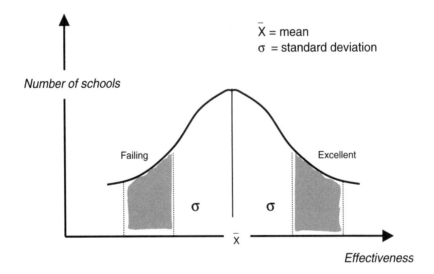

Figure 5.4 Normal distribution of effective schools.

reports ('pandas'), which allow comparisons to be made between schools with similar social catchments. Pandas work on the assumption that the socio-economic profile of a school's catchment gives a 'proxy indication' of prior attainment.

Since business benchmarking is not norm-referenced, there is no need to take extraneous factors into account. Instead, characteristics of the product and its sale (such as price, utility value, marketing and shop opening hours) are adjusted to suit the market, in the hope that equal success will be achieved across all catchment areas. Since the intended output is the same in all catchments, benchmarking concentrates on process, unlike education, where the characteristics of effectiveness are adjusted to suit the catchment area and benchmarking concentrates on output.

Threats to benchmarking improvements

There is no evidence that, in isolation, target-setting and measuring effectiveness actually improve performance, although one might be excused for making that assumption. In fact, some influential writers on quality control in industrial production have denied that measuring productivity leads to any improvement and have consequently recommended that quality needs to be built into process rather than output (Deming, 1986). In many ways, this is an argument about management versus leadership – a familiar theme to those who work in education. It is not an argument about whether benchmarking is worthwhile or not. Comparative benchmarking is not about measurement in isolation, whether process or output; nor is it solely about target-setting. It is about using information from both measurement and target-setting, in both process and output, to improve performance. It has the added bonus that knowing how critical processes are conducted in more effective organisations is a powerful incentive, in a way that 'statistical' benchmarking against national expectations or localised averages is not.

Schools and colleges can be conservative places, fearful of change, and changing the way things are done can be a difficult process even in organisations where staff recognise the need for it. The challenge of comparative benchmarking lies in its tripartite approach.

- Comparative benchmarking forces a recognition that similar critical processes are performed better elsewhere and that therefore, the home institution is inferior in some way.
- Comparative benchmarking challenges the way effectiveness is measured by comparing against the best (or at least the better), rather than against a calculated normative median.
- Comparative benchmarking forces change.

Implementing change in benchmarking organisations has the advantage that the centre has already accepted the need for change by the very act of undertaking the benchmarking process. This is not to say that all resistance has been overcome. All organisations have, to a greater or lesser extent, a natural inertia, which is sometimes made manifest by a pride in what is perceived to be stability. This can threaten the implementation of benchmarking improvements, as can the following:

- Disagreement at senior management level.

- Lack of clear recommendations emerging from the benchmarking process.
- Benchmarking recommendations that are overly complicated.
- Gain that is not perceived as being commensurate with the 'pain'.
- Lack of resources – financial or otherwise.

Most of these problems can be overcome by careful planning at the early stages. Certainly, if the agreement of senior managers was obtained prior to the benchmarking process, as it should have been, then subsequent disagreement should not be a frequently occurring problem.

The most fundamental principle that needs agreement between senior management and the benchmarking team, is that the process of benchmarking is not simply gathering information on how critical processes are carried out elsewhere. It is not educational espionage. Comparative benchmarking should be the driving force behind a continuous ongoing cycle of improvement, of which data collection is only one part. This tenet must be agreed from the outset and restated regularly by the benchmarking team. It should underpin all subsequent decisions and recommendations. There can be no compromise on the necessity to link benchmarking with change and it should be incorporated into a mission statement for the benchmarking team.

The selection of a good benchmarking team within the school or college, coupled with proper training for participating staff, should counter the threat of overly complicated recommendations at the end of the benchmarking process. Similarly, the benchmarking team, under astute leadership, should be aware throughout the process of the need to balance pain with gain. While a certain amount of each is inevitable, the objective should be to maximise the latter and minimise the former. In other words, the benchmarking process itself should be efficient in order to be effective.

The most critical and common threat to implementing recommended changes from benchmarking usually comes from inadequate resourcing. With the best will in the world, senior management may find itself unable to resource the recommendations fully. The benchmarking process itself will have taken some time to complete and in that time, circumstances may have changed for the school or college concerned. The senior management team may have originally set aside a fairly generous budget for implementing the resulting changes, but in the interim may have been faced with emergency costs that could not have been predicted. There is little that can be done in such circumstances and the only recommendation that can be made here, is that the benchmarkers be as patient as professional integrity allows. Assuming that the senior management team is genuine about its desire to seek improvement through benchmarking, the outcomes will be revisited sooner rather than later. As long as the intervening period is not too great, nothing significant will have been lost as a result of the delay. The credibility of the benchmarking process among non-participating staff will not have suffered unduly either – teachers have come to expect delays in the implementation of reform. What is more important is that the benchmarking team does not compromise on what needs to be done to effect major improvement. It is not advisable to accept resourcing of half-measures as a surrogate. Half-measures will only reduce the gradient of the improvement curve (see Figure 4.1) to the extent that the reduction in 'gain' will adversely affect the ratio to 'pain'. In addition, the performance gap between the actual and the desired will not have been reduced. It is far better to wait for full resourcing and full implementation.

The time-frame for benchmarking and communicating outcomes

Typically, comparative benchmarking for a school or Further Education college takes the greater part of an academic year (see Figure 5.5). This can vary of course, depending on the number of participating organisations in the benchmarking consortium, the type of benchmarking used and the number of critical processes involved. Planning should be done during the summer vacation immediately preceding the start of active benchmarking. Typically, dissemination to staff will then take place during the final term, after

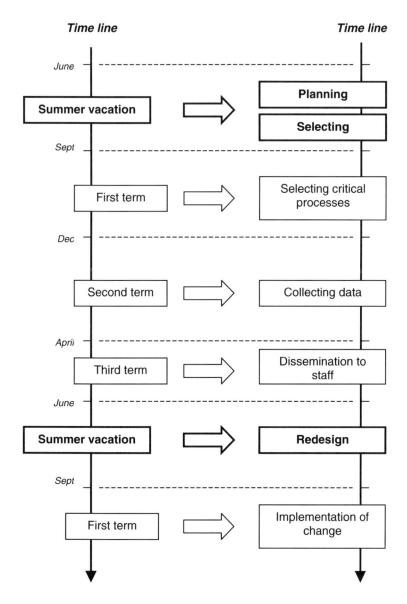

Figure 5.5 Timetable for benchmarking.

one year's benchmarking, and the intention should be to plan the implementation of change during the following summer vacation. Figure 5.5 shows a realistic time-line.

The issue of communicating recommendations from the benchmarking team to the senior management team is a serious one. In all probability, some managers will feel threatened by the findings, while others will feel that they have been singled out for criticism – which may or may not be true. Either way, communication should be thorough and dispassionate. Since a large group makes for a more threatening encounter, it is better if the presentation of recommendations is made by the benchmarking team leader, with some assistance from a 'technical' (accounts, statistics, etc.) colleague perhaps. If any of the recommendations are particularly critical or contentious, the head or principal should have first sight of the report. In extreme cases, it may even be necessary to present some findings to senior line managers on an individual basis.

As far as presentation to the rest of the staff is concerned, it is good practice to present a report at a staff day or at a specially convened staff meeting. As the cycle of redesign and improvement gets under way, it will be necessary to produce a regular information bulletin and make full use of the staff noticeboard. To prevent benchmarking fatigue, regular feedback should be given to staff and it should be as positive and reinforcing as possible. All measured gains in effectiveness, no matter how small, should be reported. Awareness and feedback are crucially important and the communications process itself needs to be quality assured. Increased effectiveness is not a success unless it is perceived as such.

Summary

- Chapter 5 was essentially concerned with the implementation of reforms brought about by the process of comparative benchmarking.
- Target-setting in schools was shown to differ in six respects from target-setting in commercial organisations:

  - the nature of the stakeholders;
  - the operating paradigm;
  - the way effectiveness was defined, achieved and measured; and
  - the way extraneous factors were dealt with as part of inspection.

- Various factors which have been shown to influence school effectiveness were discussed as a set of limits on the freedom of managers to manage.
- Threats to implementing benchmarking reforms and how to overcome them, a realistic time-frame for delivery, and recommendations for dissemination were also discussed.

6 Target-setting tables and benchmarking charts

Target-setting can be used in any and every aspect of school life, from teaching and learning to building maintenance. It forms the penultimate stage of the benchmarking process – bringing to the home organisation what others do more effectively. Target-setting is the plan by which the organisation hopes to move up the improvement curve (see Figure 4.1).

Most targets are 'threshold' measurements. A level is set, the organisation aims to meet or exceed it, and the extent to which the level is reached or exceeded is taken as a measure of effectiveness. Clearly, setting the desired levels of attainment is the critical thing. They need to be specific, measurable, achievable, relevant, time-framed and agreed (s.m.a.r.t.a.) (Zairi, 1996; DfEE, 1997a). They need to be challenging, but not dispiriting, and depend to a large extent on getting the correct proportion *not* to achieve.

In theory, threshold targets are criterion-referenced, but of course, they become norm-referenced when adjusted so that a certain percentage fails. If targets are achieved too easily, the level is, by definition, too low. If too few achieve the targets, the level is too high.

The DfEE have identified four 'target zones' for benchmarking (DfEE, 1997b) (Figure 6.1).

- Cautious targets are in the 'historic zone' and are used in situations where staff feels threatened. They are often less ambitious than even current achievement levels and usually result in lower standards.
- Readily achievable targets are said to be in the 'comfort zone' and reflect a low priority.
- The 'challenge zone' has high priority targets which, if achieved, will make a significant difference to performance.
- Targets in the 'unlikely zone' are used as emergency measures, but commonly fail to be achieved, creating disappointment and undermining improvement strategies.

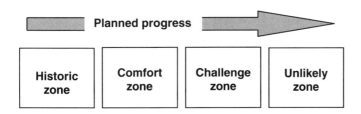

Figure 6.1 Target zones. (After DfEE, 1997b.)

Targets in the comfort zone lead to small incremental improvements in effectiveness (see Figure 3.1), whereas targets in the challenge zone lead to radical step-gains in effectiveness (see Figure 3.2), designed to close the performance gap on comparable institutions (see Figure 4.1).

Whatever the nature of the targets themselves, the process of setting them can be most easily handled if each critical process is divided into four general components: input; process; output, and consequence (Figure 6.2).

- An 'input target' is one which states what will be done and why, in general terms.
- A 'process target' is one that states how, when and who will perform specific functions.
- An 'output target' states what the organisation hopes to achieve in measurable terms.
- A 'consequence target' can be thought of as a desirable outcome and relates to the context within which the school or college operates.

More often than not, these four components are well defined, but sometimes they are not. An example will illustrate the difference (Figure 6.3).

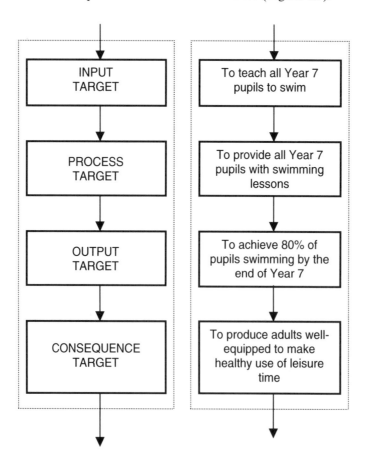

Figure 6.2 Types of target.   *Figure 6.3* Example.

- Aiming to teach all Year Seven pupils to swim, as part of their Physical Education programme, is an input target.
- Providing all Year Seven pupils with a series of ten swimming lessons in their first term at school is a process target.
- Aiming for an 80 per cent success rate is an output target.
- Producing health-conscious young adults who are well equipped to make full use of their leisure time is a consequence target.

Tables 6.1 to 6.28 below show input, process, output and consequence targets under the following headings:

❑ Managing the curriculum and teaching (Tables 6.1–6.4)

❑ Discipline (Tables 6.5–6.8)

❑ Leadership (Tables 6.9–6.12)

❑ Managing personnel and staff development (Tables 6.13–6.16)

❑ Managing external and customer relations (Tables 6.17–6.20)

❑ Managing the built environment (Tables 6.21–6.24)

❑ Managing finance (Tables 6.25–6.28)

The tables are based on what school effectiveness research tells us makes for a good school (see Figure 5.2). Benchmarkers may find them useful starting points for examining important critical processes and again later for setting targets for improvement. They are not intended to be exhaustive or prescriptive.

The first line on each table is filled in as an example. They have been coded in such a way that the progress of any one target can be followed through all four stages. For example, Input Target **Im12** on Table 1, becomes Process Target **Pm12** on Table 2, then Output Target **Om12** on Table 3 and finally Consequence Target **Cm12** on Table 4 (m = 'managing the curriculum').

The Appendix contains Charts 1 to 28, which can be used for comparative benchmarking for up to three schools or colleges. They have been designed to match Tables 6.1 to 6.28 and benchmarkers can use them to gather and compare data from consortium partners. Again, they are not intended to be exhaustive, but are arranged under the same headings for convenience:

❑ Managing the curriculum and teaching (Charts 1–4)

❑ Discipline (Charts 5–8)

❑ Leadership (Charts 9–12)

❑ Managing personnel and staff development (Charts 13–16)

❑ Managing external and customer relations (Charts 17–20)

❑ Managing the built environment (Charts 21–24)

❑ Managing finance (Charts 25–28)

Target-setting for managing the curriculum and teaching

The term 'curriculum' means different things to different people. Some take it to mean a set of syllabuses or specifications; others take it to mean the sum of all pupil experiences in school or college. What the school or college defines as curriculum will depend on the ethos and philosophical tradition of the institution – liberal, progressive, vocational or cultural (Barber, 1996) – and the targets set for teachers will largely depend on it too. However, most schools and colleges work to a common agenda, whether it is the National Curriculum or standards set by an awarding or examination body. These syllabuses or specifications are set down and teachers work to find the best ways of achieving the desired output. Measuring teacher effectiveness therefore, like pupil assessment, partly involves testing pupils as to the extent to which they have achieved these pre-ordained objectives.

Research indicates the importance of sensible arrangements for teaching and learning in schools. The following is a brief synopsis.

- Time spent on instruction is maximised in high achieving schools (Alexander, 1997; Rutter *et al.*, 1979; Bennett, 1992) and there is high curriculum coverage (Tizard *et al.*, 1988; Bennett, 1992).
- Students in low achieving schools often work on their own as teachers attend to administration (Good and Brophy, 1986).
- High achieving schools have high expectations of students, who perceive that teachers are pushing them academically (Teddlie and Stringfield, 1993). Teaching is intellectually challenging, stimulating and enthusiastic, with a high incidence of higher order questions (Mortimore *et al.*, 1988).
- Teachers in low achieving schools tend to reinforce what is *not* done well (Good and Brophy, 1986).
- There is mobility between groupings/streams/sets in high achieving schools (Good and Brophy, 1986).
- Team learning is emphasised in high achieving schools (Good and Brophy, 1986) and the general climate is one of concern for excellence (Teddlie and Stringfield, 1993; Sammons, Hillman and Mortimore, 1995).
- Teachers in low achieving schools make unrealistic assessments of current student achievement (Teddlie and Stringfield, 1993), and tracking and monitoring systems for student progress are less effective (Mortimore *et al.*, 1988; Levine and Lezotte, 1990; Sammons, Hillman and Mortimore, 1995).
- In effective schools, teaching is firm, purposeful and consistent (Rutter *et al.*, 1979; Good and Brophy, 1986; Mortimore *et al.*, 1988; Scheerens, 1992).
- In effective schools, learning is structured, flexible and well organised (Rutter *et al.*, 1979; Mortimore *et al.*, 1988; Scheerens, 1992). Negative effects are found when pupils are given unlimited responsibility for a long list of tasks (Mortimore *et al.*, 1988).

Table 6.1 Examples of input targets for teaching and managing the curriculum

Code	INPUT TARGETS FOR MANAGING THE CURRICULUM AND TEACHING	Yes/No	ZONE			
			Historic	Comfort	Challenge	Unlikely
I m 1	Does the curriculum meets statutory requirements?	Y		•		
I m 2	Is there equality of opportunity for students (race, creed, gender, etc.)?					
I m 3	Do teachers make the curriculum relevant to the needs of students?					
I m 4	Does the school fulfil its obligations to students with special needs?					
I m 5	Does the school offer subject progression for students post-16?					
I m 6	Does the curriculum prepare students for work and HE?					
I m 7	Does the curriculum promote spiritual, moral and cultural development?					
I m 8	Does the curriculum promote physical development?					
I m 9	Does the school provide personal, social and health education?					
I m 10	Does the school have adequate policies for curriculum areas?					
I m 11	Do teachers implement the school's curriculum policy?					
I m 12	Does the school have a policy on the class sizes?					
I m 13	Is the school staffed in such a way as to ensure that the curriculum is delivered?					
I m 14	Is there adequate subject choice for students?					
I m 15	Is there careers advice for students?					

I t 1	Do teachers have high expectations of students?					
I t 2	Are lessons challenging to pupils?					
I t 3	Do teachers encourage achievement?					
I t 4	Are lessons generally well-structured?					
I t 5	Is teaching generally flexible?					
I t 6	Is teaching generally purposeful?					
I t 7	Is class-contact time maximised?					
I t 8	Is student progress monitored sufficiently by teachers?					
I t 9	Is there effective and regular student assessment by teachers?					
I t 10	Do teachers predict public examination results accurately?					
I t 11	Is there adequate curricular support for students (study and library facilities)?					
I t 12	Is there a programme of extra-curricular and sporting activities?					
I t 13	Does the school have a policy on extra-curricular activities and interference with classroom teaching?					
I t 14	Does the school canvas student and parent opinion on the curriculum?					
I t 15	Is information about the curriculum communicated to students and parents?					

Table 6.2 Examples of process targets for teaching and managing the curriculum

Code	PROCESS TARGETS FOR MANAGING THE CURRICULUM AND TEACHING	Target no. of times, % p.a. or amount	ZONE			
			Historic	Comfort	Challenge	Unlikely
P m 1	The curriculum group meets...*(monthly)*...	(10)			•	
P m 2	The group reviewing equality of opportunity meets					
P m 3	All students receive ICT instruction every					
P m 4	The group reviewing special needs meets					
P m 5	The curriculum group and careers advisors meet					
P m 6	Careers advisors and employers meet					
P m 7	Years 7–11 have a module on culture and spirituality for ....hrs/week for..........weeks					
P m 8	All students do PE and take part at least .... activities					
P m 9	All students take a module on personal, social and health education for..........hrs/week for..........weeks					
P m 10	The curriculum group consults staff..........					
P m 11	Heads of Dept. instruct staff .... as to curriculum policy					
P m 12	The PTR for KS3 classes is.......... The PTR for KS4 classes is.......... The PTR for post-16 classes is..........The average PTR is ....The average number of students per practical class is..........					
P m 13	Heads of Dept. give staffing requirements to the curriculum group every					
P m 14	The curriculum group and careers advisors meet every					
P m 15	A student meets a career advisor formally at least .... in Year 13					

P t 1	Teachers are reminded .... to have high expectations					
P t 2	Students are entered for .... challenges and competitions					
P t 3	Teachers are reminded .... to encourage excellence					
P t 4	Teacher lesson plans are inspected by Heads of Dept.					
P t 5	Teacher lesson plans are inspected by Heads of Dept.					
P t 6	Teacher lesson plans are inspected by Heads of Dept.					
P t 7	The Contact Ratio is..........Teachers are late on fewer than .... occasions and absent on fewer than..........occasions					
P t 8	Teacher records of student progress are inspected .... by Heads of Dept. Parent-teacher meetings are held every..........					
P t 9	Students have formal house exams .... annually					
P t 10	Teachers make formal predictions on..........occasions of exam results for Years 11 and 13					
P t 11	The library and study hall are open from..........to..........on..........					
P t 12	The activities programme contains a range of .... options					
P t 13	Years 11 and 13 do not participate in					
P t 14	The school canvases student and parent opinion every					
P t 15	The Newsletter gives information on curriculum issues and is issued					

Table 6.3 Examples of output targets for teaching and managing the curriculum

Code	OUTPUT TARGETS FOR MANAGING THE CURRICULUM AND TEACHING	Target no. of times, % p.a. or amount	ZONE			
			Historic	Comfort	Challenge	Unlikely
O m 1	The curriculum group produces..........reports annually	1	•			
	..........% of students are entered for English, Maths and Science	98%	•			
	..........% obtain grades A-C in all three	47%			•	
	..........% obtain grades A-G in all three	93%				•
O m 2	The group reviewing equality of opportunity finds that..........% of subjects are taken equally by boys and girls to within ....%					
O m 3	..........% of students obtain Level..........in IT key skills					
O m 4	The group reviewing special needs finds that ....% of students have ....% of their needs met adequately					
O m 5	The curriculum group find that..........% of students are content that all their subject requirements are being met					
	..........% of students go on to Further Education and training					
	..........% of students go on to Higher Education					
	..........% of students go on to employment					
O m 6	..........% of students obtain the key skills qualification (Levels..........)					
	..........% of students not progressing to FE/HE obtain employment					
O m 7	..........% of students attend at least..........cultural events and ....% go on school outings					
O m 8	..........% of students take two activities					
O m 9	..........% of students express themselves satisfied that the PSHE module addressed their needs					
O m 10	..........% of subject areas have adequate policies					
O m 11	..........% of teachers are aware of curriculum policy					
O m 12	The average class size is.......... and ....% have less than.......... ....% of KS3 classes have a PTR of....... ....% of KS4 classes have a PTR of........ ....% of post-16 classes have a PTR of........					
O m 13	..........% of subjects have adequate cover					
O m 14	..........% of students have no subject clashes; ....% have one					
O m 15	..........% of students meet the careers advisor ....times					
O t 1	..........% of students will obtain grades A–C in each subject					
	..........% of students will obtain grades A–C in 5 or more subjects					
	..........% of students will obtain grades A–G in 5 or more subjects					
	..........% of students will obtain grades A–G in 1 or more subjects					
	Ofsted rates..........% of lessons inspected as good or better.					
O t 2	..........% of students will compete in an academic challenge/activity					
O t 3	..........% of subjects have..........% of A/A* grades at..........exam					
	..........% of students are entered for 2 or more A-levels					
	..........% of students obtain grades A–C in 2 or more A-levels					
	The average A-level points per candidate is..........					
O t 4	..........% of lesson plans in each subject will be on time, as scheduled					
O t 5	..........% of lesson plans in each subject will have adjusted successfully to unforeseen interferences in the year plan					
O t 6	..........% of lesson plans in each subject will have a stated aim					
O t 7	..........% of teachers are late on fewer than.......... occasions ....% of teachers are absent zero days and ....% are absent without certification on fewer than..........occasions the number of hours instruction per week is..........					
O t 8	..........% of instances showing poor pupil progress will have been reported to tutors by teachers and will have been followed up. There is a minimum of..........parent-teacher meetings every year					
O t 9	Written reports to parents will be sent within..........days (of exams)					
O t 10	..........% of teachers predict..........exam results to within ....%					
O t 11	The library and study hall are used by..........students regularly					
O t 12	..........% of students avail of..........% of extra curricular activities					
O t 13	..........% of teachers are satisfied that extra curricular activities do not interfere with exam preparation					
O t 14	..........% of students and ....% of parents will express themselves satisfied with teaching and the curriculum					
O t 15	..........% of parents will express themselves satisfied with the level of communication with the school					

Table 6.4 Examples of consequence targets for teaching and managing the curriculum

Code	CONSEQUENCE TARGETS FOR MANAGING THE CURRICULUM AND TEACHING	Does the school regard this target as desirable? Y/N	Low priority	Mid priority	High priority
C m 1	Students are equipped to meet society's needs	Y	•		
C m 2	Former and current students have an awareness of equality issues				
C m 3	Students perceive education as relevant				
C m 4	The school cherishes all its pupils equally				
C m 5	Students perceive education as useful				
C m 6	Former students are successful				
C m 7	Students leave with cultural and spiritual values				
C m 8	Students are health conscious				
C m 9	Students are prepared to make informed decisions about personal and social choices				
C m 10	The school is reflective about its mission				
C m 11	Teachers in the school are reflective practitioners				
C m 12	Students receive individual attention at the school				
C m 13	The school is stable yet flexible				
C m 14	Students are well-prepared for HE and employment competition				
C m 15	Students are well-advised and career focused				

C t 1	The school has a high retention rate				
C t 2	The school can look after pupils of all abilities				
C t 3	The school acknowledges pupil achievement				
C t 4	The school is well-organised and inspection reports are good				
C t 5	Teaching is varied and interesting				
C t 6	The school team has a shared sense of purpose				
C t 7	The school is an efficient and effective place of work				
C t 8	The school encourages a partnership between home and school				
C t 9	The school is aware and alert				
C t 10	Teachers give informed advice to parents and students				
C t 11	The school supports ambitious students				
C t 12	Past students are well-prepared to make constructive use of their leisure time				
C t 13	Achievement and prioritisation are valued				
C t 14	Customers are in touch with the school				
C t 15	The school is in touch with its customers				

Target-setting for discipline

Maintaining effective classroom learning environments is a feature of effective schools (Creemers, 1994) and emphasising student responsibility increases the chance of students acquiring the school's values and developing a commitment to learning (Reynolds and Murgatroyd, 1977; Rutter *et al.*, 1979). School effectiveness research also indicates that:

- Effective schools maintain an orderly environment (Rutter *et al.*, 1979; Lezotte, 1989; Sammons, Hillman and Mortimore, 1995) with an adequate system of reward, praise and appreciation (Rutter *et al.*, 1979).
- In effective schools, good behaviour is reinforced (Rutter *et al.*, 1979; Mortimore *et al.*, 1988) and teachers are good role models for behaviour (Rutter *et al.*, 1979).
- In effective schools, students are given responsibility (Rutter *et al.*, 1979) and are held in high esteem (Reynolds and Murgatroyd, 1977; Mortimore *et al.*, 1988; Levine and Lezotte, 1990; Sammons, Hillman and Mortimore, 1995). There are high levels of pupil involvement in extra curricular activities and there are occasional 'truces' on the imposition of certain rules (Reynolds, 1976).
- Discipline in effective schools is based on a combination of firm leadership and teacher involvement and is perceived as fair, transparent and responsive (Rutter *et al.*, 1979; Mortimore *et al.*, 1988; Sammons, Hillman and Mortimore, 1995).
- There is a work-centred ethos in effective schools, characterised by a high level of student industry, low noise levels and a minimum of movement about classrooms (Mortimore *et al.*, 1988).

Table 6.5 Examples of input targets for discipline

Code	INPUT TARGETS FOR DISCIPLINE	Yes/No	ZONE Historic	Comfort	Challenge	Unlikely
I d 1	Does the school have an appropriate system of reward and punishment?	Y	•			
I d 2	Does the school have a discipline policy statement?					
I d 3	Are students and parents made aware of the discipline policy?					
I d 4	Is there an orderly atmosphere in the school?					
I d 5	Is there an orderly atmosphere in classrooms?					
I d 6	Is the discipline system responsive and sensitive to circumstances?					
I d 7	Do parents and students perceive the system as impartial and transparent?					
I d 8	Is good behaviour reinforced?					
I d 9	Are students given responsibility?					
I d 10	Are students held in high esteem by teachers?					
I d 11	Are teachers held in high esteem by students?					

Table 6.6 Examples of process targets for discipline

Code	PROCESS TARGETS FOR DISCIPLINE	Target no. of times, % p.a. or amount	ZONE Historic	Comfort	Challenge	Unlikely
P d 1	The system is reviewed every...*(year)*... Records are kept by...*(tutors)*...and feedback given to staff and parents every...*(week)*... Punishment ranges from...*(a talking to)*...to...*(exclusion)*...Reward ranges from...*(praise)*...to...*(scholarships)*... The...*(deputy)*...is in charge of discipline	1 / 32		• (32)	• (1)	
P d 2	Senior management informs staff every..........as to discipline policy. Policy is reviewed every.......... There is a code of conduct for staff and students. Staff use discipline appropriately					
P d 3	Students and parents are initially informed about discipline policy on .... and reminded of it					
P d 4	Tutors meet students at least every.......... At least..........teachers are on duty at break times. Reports of incidents between lessons are kept by..........and followed-up on by..........					
P d 5	Teachers meet tutors formally at least every..........					
P d 6	Staff are informed of individual student backgrounds every.......... so that they can (re)act sensibly to indiscipline					
P d 7	Parent and student satisfaction is surveyed every..........					
P d 8	Staff share a common system of rewards and prizes for both effort and achievement. Rewards are acknowledged every.......... The system is reviewed every..........					
P d 9	There is a general student forum and a prefects forum and they meet every.......... Students participate in the selection of prefects every..........					
P d 10	Teachers address students by first names and speak to them outside lessons. Negative comment in the staffroom is rare					
P d 11	Students speak highly of their teachers and speak respectfully to them between lessons					

Table 6.7 Examples of output targets for discipline

Code	OUTPUT TARGETS FOR DISCIPLINE	Target no. of times, % p.a. or amount	ZONE Historic	ZONE Comfort	ZONE Challenge	ZONE Unlikely
O d 1	The average number of commendations per teacher per cohort is.......... and the average number of sanctions per teacher per cohort is.......... The greatest number of sanctions used by a teacher is..........and the range is from..........to.......... ....% of teachers used fewer than..........sanctions. There are..........whole-school assemblies	20 7 10 0–15 75% 4 32	•	•	• • • •	•
O d 2	The number of management-staff disputes over inappropriate use of sanctions and rewards is..........					
O d 3	The number of parent complaints is.......... The number of student complaints is..........					
O d 4	The number of reported incidents from teachers to tutors is.......... The number of internal suspensions is.......... The number of external suspensions is.......... The number of exclusions is .... The number of incidents of vandalism is..........					
O d 5	..........% of reported incidents from teachers is classroom-based ....% of internal suspensions is classroom-based ....% of internal suspensions is classroom-based ....% of exclusions is classroom-based					
O d 6	..........% of parents requested to attend a meeting in the school attend. ....% of suspensions/exclusions come from socially disadvantaged pupils.					
O d 7	..........% of parents surveyed express themselves content ....% of students surveyed express themselves content					
O d 8	..........% of students obtain at least one commendation/reward for good behaviour					
O d 9	..........% of students are given at least.......positions of responsibility					
O d 10	..........% of teachers involve themselves in extra-curricular activities					
O d 11	..........% of teachers think that students respect them. The number of incidents of threatening behaviour towards is..........					

Table 6.8 Examples of consequence targets for discipline

Code	CONSEQUENCE TARGETS FOR DISCIPLINE	Does the school regard this target as desirable?	Low priority	Mid priority	High priority
C d 1	Students respect the rights of others	Y			•
C d 2	Students appreciate openness				
C d 3	Responsibility for discipline is shared between home and school				
C d 4	Students appreciate the necessity for orderliness				
C d 5	Students value constructive participation and tolerance				
C d 6	Students regard school as a refuge				
C d 7	Students appreciate fairness				
C d 8	Students learn that incentive (as opposed to threat) can reap rewards				
C d 9	Students appreciate responsibility				
C d 10	Students learn how to earn respect				
C d 11	Students learn to respect others				

Target-setting for leadership

Most studies on school effectiveness show that transformational leadership by the head or principal, a shared sense of vision and a participative approach to staff involvement are all features of effective schools (Reynolds and Teddlie, 2000).

'Vision' is the mental picture of a preferred future. It shapes policies, programmes, plans and priorities, and in effective schools, is shared with the wider school community (Bennis and Nanus, 1985). In effective schools, the head or principal institutionalises this vision and uses it to illuminate the ordinary with 'dramatic significance' (Beare, Caldwell and Millikan, 1997).

'Leadership' is more difficult to define, but a number of characteristics have been noted over the course of many studies. Dubin (1961) defined leadership simply as the exercise of authority whereas Stogdill and Bass (1981) defined it as the process of influencing the activities of an organised group towards setting and accomplishing goals. This latter view acknowledges that people without formal authority may be leaders (e.g. a much admired, but little promoted teacher) and suggests that leadership is not about the maintenance of an existing system – that is management – but about initiating change. Good leadership makes clear the reasons for change and makes it meaningful in an organisational sense. Leaders try to commit others to the values they espouse and build their organisations on the unification of people around those values (Sergiovanni, 1992).

Among the traits exhibited by successful leaders are: a concern for task completion; energy; persistence; originality; self-confidence; a willingness to take risks; a capacity to influence others; a capacity to handle stress; and a sense of concern for others (Stogdill and Bass, 1981). These dual concerns for accomplishing tasks and building good relationships with people are often seen as opposite extremes of a continuum and two notable contingency theories have been developed around this polarity.

The first holds that leadership behaviour should be varied according to the maturity of subordinates (Hersey and Blanchard, 1982) and that there are four leadership types for four degrees of maturity, as Figure 6.4 illustrates (leadership styles go anti-clockwise from 'telling' to 'delegating', as organisational maturity increases).

The second contingency theory distinguishes between leadership behaviour and leadership style (Fiedler, 1967). 'Style' is an innate aspect of personality and determines orientation when exercising leadership. 'Behaviour', on the other hand, is a set of actions that the leader may choose to perform or not. The theory holds that task-motivated leaders are most effective in situations that are highly favourable or highly unfavourable (as determined by whether the tasks are structured or unstructured, whether relationships are good or bad and whether the leader has a position of power or not); and relationship-motivated leaders are most effective when situations are moderately favourable or moderately unfavourable.

Modern 'transformational' theories of leadership, such as those of Senge (1990, 1999), Bennis (1985) and Gardner (1996), suggest that effective headship should seek to satisfy the higher needs of teaching staff. The relationship should be one of mutual stimulation – teachers should have the opportunity to act in leadership roles and leaders

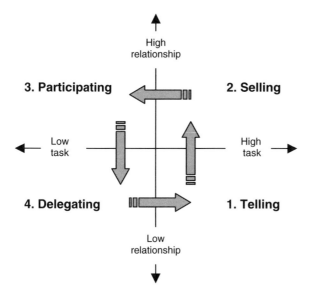

Figure 6.4 Leadership styles.

the opportunity to become 'moral agents' (Burns, 1978). Typically, in such schools, teachers are generous with their time and managers are concerned with promoting a culture where excellence is valued and rewarded.

The culture of the effective school or college is also characterised by value slogans, enhanced status for heroes who embody the values of the school, rituals in which shared values are experienced and heroes celebrated, induction stories about values or heroes who triumphed in the face of adversity, and networks of people who protect successful practices (Beare, Caldwell and Millikan, 1997). Other characteristics include:

- Firm, purposeful and supportive leadership (Mortimore *et al.*, 1988; Hopkins, Ainscow and West, 1994; Sammons, Thomas and Mortimore, 1997).
- Adequate staff monitoring. In low achieving schools, the head is primarily an administrator and disciplinarian who seldom visits classrooms (Teddlie and String-field, 1993) and there is little by way of instructional leadership (Levine and Lezotte, 1990; Louis and Miles, 1990).
- A positive, pleasant and encouraging atmosphere (Mortimore *et al.*, 1988; Hopkins, Ainscow and West, 1994; Stoll and Fink, 1994). Low achieving schools are charac-terised by a negative climate (Teddlie and Stringfield, 1993).
- A shared sense of vision, unity of purpose and a sense of collegiality (Levine and Lezotte, 1990; Louis and Miles, 1990; Fullan, 1991; Hopkins, Ainscow and West, 1994; Sammons, Hillman and Mortimore, 1995).
- The involvement of middle managers in decision-making and the sharing of academic leadership (Teddlie and Stringfield, 1993).

Table 6.9 Examples of input targets for leadership

Code	INPUT TARGETS FOR LEADERSHIP	Yes/No	Historic	Comfort	Challenge	Unlikely
I L 1	Is leadership transforming, rather than transactional?	Y			•	
	Are 'end' values important and not just 'modal' ones?	Y			•	
I L 2	Do senior managers have a vision for the school and do they articulate/communicate it to staff?					
I L 3	Do staff share management's vision and do senior managers take staff with them?					
I L 4	Does the vision permeate everyday activities in the school?					
I L 5	Is the vision implanted in the structures and processes of the school? Do senior managers develop a 'culture' in the school?					
I L 6	Is there a staff induction programme? Do managers have high expectations of staff?					
I L 7	Do senior managers encourage collaborative decision-making?					
I L 8	Are staff involved in curriculum decision-making? Are staff involved in resource decision-making?					
I L 9	Are responsibilities/duties shared across the school?					
I L 10	Is staff self-esteem high? Do managers build and maintain morale?					
I L 11	Has management the capacity to plan, organise and co-ordinate?					

Table 6.10 Examples of process targets for leadership

Code	PROCESS TARGETS FOR LEADERSHIP	Target no. of times, % p.a. or amount	ZONE			
			Historic	Comfort	Challenge	Unlikely
P L 1	Teachers are prepared for leadership by rotating duties every......... and involving staff in forming policy on at least .... occasions. Managers look past immediate measurements of effectiveness	3 yrs 1	•		• •	
P L 2	Senior management informs staff every..........as to its vision of the future. Policy is reviewed every..........and involves staff. There is continuous clarification, consensus-seeking and commitment					
P L 3	Staff spend an average of..........hours in over-time contributing to the mission. Staff opinion is sought in relation to where the school is going every..........					
P L 4	Activities are reviewed every..........in relation to creating a preferred future. Policies are formulated with the mission in mind and are displayed.......... and communicated to parents every.......... Aspects of the vision are communicated to students every..........					
P L 5	There are assemblies every..........taken by the.......... There are..........annual celebration events used to reinforce the vision The vision and ethos is referred to in promotional literature Staff are encouraged to be creative in thinking of ways in which the vision can be reinforced by structures, events and processes					
P L 6	New and promoted staff are inducted by the..........for..........days. Their satisfaction with the induction programme is surveyed in retrospect					
P L 7	Participation and collaboration is spontaneous, but there is an open system for communicating the results to management					
P L 8	There are staff groupings involved with decision-making in relation to the curriculum and resource allocation. The groups meet every ....and report to senior management every..........					
P L 9	There are staff teams in..........areas, each with an average of.......... members. They meet..........times per term					
P L 10	Teachers are praised publicly for their achievements. Successful teachers are perceived to embody the values of the school and there are rituals where their reward is made public					
P L 11	The management is perceived as efficient					

Table 6.11 Examples of output targets for leadership

Code	OUTPUT TARGETS FOR LEADERSHIP	Target no. of times, % p.a. or amount	ZONE			
			Historic	Comfort	Challenge	Unlikely
O L 1	..........% of budget is given to staff leadership development	10%			•	
	..........% of staff are promoted every..........years	5% 3yrs				•
	..........% of policies refer to end values, like 'excellence'	100%		•		
O L 2	..........% of staff are involved in policy-making. Staff meetings are held every.......... and..........% of staff attend					
O L 3	..........% of staff agree with management's vision ....% of staff are involved in management related activities ....% stay in school voluntarily more than..........times per term					
O L 4	Policies are reviewed every..........by governors There are..........assemblies every term for each cohort Copies are given to parents/students at.......... and the vision is communicated to parents in the Newsletter every..........					
O L 5	..........% of assemblies are used to reinforce the vision and ethos ....% of staff take part in assembly at least.......... ....% of staff take part in annual celebration events ....% of staff contribute to promotional activities					
O L 6	..........% of new and promoted staff are inducted and..........% express themselves content with the induction, one year on					
O L 7	..........% of staff participate in..........(area) decision-making ....% of recommendations from staff teams are adopted					
O L 8	..........% participate in curriculum decision-making and ....% in the allocation of resources. Attendance at these meetings averages ....%					
O L 9	..........% of staff participate in staff teams Attendance at meetings averages..........%					
O L 10	Less than ....% of permanent staff leave for another school, except for promotion Staff achievement is acknowledged formally on..........occasions					
O L 11	The management team is praised by inspectors and governors for their organisational skills There are fewer than..........event clashes per term and more than......... planning events attended by..........% of staff Teachers know their teaching duties for the following year/term .... weeks in advance					

Table 6.12 Examples of consequence targets for leadership

Code	CONSEQUENCE TARGETS FOR LEADERSHIP	Does the school regard this target as desirable?	Low priority	Mid priority	High priority
C L 1	The school is well-prepared to meet future challenges	Y	•		
C L 2	The school progresses as a community. Improvement is expected				
C L 3	Staff give freely of their time. Absence and tardiness are kept to a minimum				
C L 4	Staff, governors, parents and students act as partners in the education process				
C L 5	The pursuit of excellence is expected and supported				
C L 6	The school attracts good teachers				
C L 7	Staff are content and professionally satisfied				
C L 8	Staff are developed professionally				
C L 9	Staff work hard and are challenged professionally				
C L 10	The school retains and rewards good teachers				
C L 11	The school presents value for money				

Target-setting for managing personnel and staff development

Whereas 'staffing' refers to full-time or part-time paid employees and probably accounts for more than three-quarters of the school budget, 'personnel' is a wider term which includes supply teachers, temporary staff, contractors and trainee teachers. The real cost to the organisation of managing personnel is high, since school and college managers spend a considerable amount of their own time dealing with those who carry the main burden of responsibility for fulfilling the mission of the organisation.

In terms of organisational effectiveness, managing and developing staff is critical. The teaching staff is likely to be the first and main source of contact between parents and the school and as such, a confident and well-informed staff is a necessity, not a luxury. Teachers are also more 'proximal' to the student and are likely to have a greater influence on output than those who are more distant (Stringfield, 1994).

Most studies on school effectiveness include monitoring staff performance and pro-active selection, dismissal and replacement of staff as determinants (Levine and Lezotte, 1990; Bridges, 1992). Such monitoring and evaluation is a process usually characterised by short unscheduled classroom visits, high visibility and regular checks on homework by senior managers (Rutter *et al.*, 1979; Sammons, Hillman and Mortimore, 1995; Reynolds and Teddlie, 2000).

Staff development is also recognised as one of the conditions that underpins the work of successful schools and the proposition that schools do not improve unless they provide collective development opportunities is widely accepted (Ainscow *et al.*, 1994). In terms of staffing, research has revealed that effective schools are also characterised by:

- The careful selection and induction of staff in order to encourage continuity of staffing (Stringfield and Teddlie, 1987; Mortimore *et al.*, 1988; Bridges, 1992).
- A spirit of institutional learning (Sammons, Hillman and Mortimore, 1995).
- A co-ordinated approach to staff development (Mortimore *et al.*, 1988; Levine and Lezotte, 1990) and an INSET programme which is both integral and practical (Mortimore *et al.*, 1988).
- High expectations of staff (Teddlie and Stringfield, 1993; Reynolds *et al.*, 1994; Sammons, Hillman and Mortimore, 1995) and a challenging atmosphere (Mortimore *et al.*, 1988).
- The regular evaluation of performance (Hopkins, Ainscow and West, 1994).
- The involvement of staff and senior managers – in particular, deputy heads – in curriculum planning and policy (Mortimore *et al.*, 1988).

Table 6.13 Examples of input targets for managing personnel and staff development

Code	INPUT TARGETS FOR MANAGING PERSONNEL AND STAFF DEVELOPMENT	Yes/No	ZONE: Historic	ZONE: Comfort	ZONE: Challenge	ZONE: Unlikely
I s 1	Is the school staffed so as to deliver a balanced curriculum effectively?	Y		•		
I s 2	Does the school have a policy on selection, appointment, appraisal and promotion?					
I s 3	Does the school have a policy on conditions of employment, sickness, stress, dismissal and grievance procedures?					
I s 4	Does the school have a policy on school-based initial teacher training and staff development?					
I s 5	Does the school have a policy on casual and long-term teacher absence?					
I s 6	Does the school have a policy on performance pay?					
I s 7	Does the school seek to retain good teachers?					
I s 8	Does the school reduce class contact hours for staff with management duties?					
I s 9	Does the school seek to reduce the pupil:teacher ratio?					

Table 6.14 Examples of process targets for managing personnel and staff development

Code	PROCESS TARGETS FOR MANAGING PERSONNEL AND STAFF DEVELOPMENT	Target no. of times, % p.a. or amount	ZONE			
			Historic	Comfort	Challenge	Unlikely
P s 1	Staffing levels within each subject area are reviewed every .... and maintained or adjusted. A ....-year staffing plan is drawn up by the senior management team, after consultation with..........	1 year 3-year Dept. heads			• •	
P s 2	Appointments and promotions are strictly on merit. Feedback is given to unsuccessful candidates within..........weeks of .... A job description accompanies each post. Vacancies are advertised internally and externally and all appointments comply with employment legislation and are equitable and transparent. There is a minimum period of..........weeks between the advertisment and the closing date A survey of staff satisfaction is conducted every					
P s 3	Job descriptions are reviewed every.......... Sickness and absence levels are reviewed every.......... Teaching staff in dispute with senior management or undergoing a disciplinary procedure are entitled to be accompanied by a colleague or a trade union representative					
P s 4	The school facilitates initial teacher training, up to a maximum of .... in any given year. Newly-qualified teachers and those on teacher-training undergo a..........day induction. Subsequently, they are entitled to attend all staff meetings and participate fully in the professional life of the school. They are not expected to cover for absent colleagues The school undertakes to encourage staff to obtain additional qualifications relevant to teaching and ....% of budget is set aside for staff development A survey of staff satisfaction is conducted after every INSET day					
P s 5	Staff are expected to cover for absent colleagues for up to.......... days per term. Casual staff absence does not exceed..........days per term per teacher. Staff present a doctor's certificate for each period of absence exceeding..........days, or two days and a weekend The management undertake to cover long-term notified absence using supply teachers. Management have made financial provision for staff absence					
P s 6	Performance related pay follows guidelines set out by the board of governors and the agreed criteria are in force for at least .... weeks before notice of assessment is served. Feedback is given to unsuccessful applicants					
P s 7	Excellent teachers are rewarded, where possible, with security of tenure or promotion					
P s 8	A schedule is drawn up and reviewed every..........of reduced teaching hours for managerial positions					
P s 9	The pupil-teacher ratio is reviewed every..........					

Table 6.15 Examples of output targets for managing personnel and staff development

Code	OUTPUT TARGETS FOR MANAGING PERSONNEL AND STAFF DEVELOPMENT	Target no. of times, % p.a. or amount	ZONE Historic	Comfort	Challenge	Unlikely
O s 1	Of the staffing budget, ...% is spent on full-time staff and	80%	•			
	.........% on part-time staff	17%	•			
	.........% of budget is spent on staff development and training	10%				•
	The number of subject areas with fewer than three teachers is less than	4				•
O s 2	.........% of applicants receive feedback within..........weeks, ...% of promotions are internal ....% of staff express themselves satisfied with appointment and promotion procedures					
O s 3	Less than..........% of teaching days are lost due to teacher absence The number of official management-staff disputes is less than ....per..........					
O s 4	.........% of newly appointed staff stay longer than..........years ....% of staff obtain additional qualifications every..........years ....% of staff attend formal development courses every year ....% of the staff development budget is used every year There are..........INSET days every term ....% of staff express themselves satisfied with INSET events					
O s 5	..........% of budget is set aside for covering/insuring against teacher absence ....% of teachers are absent zero days ....% of teachers are absent without certification (casual) on fewer than .... occasions ....% of teaching days are lost due to uncertified illness ....% of teaching days are lost due to certified illness ....% of uncertified absence was covered by staff ....% of certified absence was covered from the outset by supply staff					
O s 6	..........% of permanent teaching staff obtain 'threshold' payments					
O s 7	The ratio of part-time to full-time staff will be..........					
O s 8	Deputies/VPs teach between..........and..........hours per week .... teach between..........and..........hours per week .... teach between..........and..........hours per week					
O s 9	The average pupil:teacher ratio is..........overall The average pupil:teacher ratio is..........for non-practical classes The number of pupils per class ranges from.......... to					

Table 6.16 Examples of consequence targets for managing personnel and staff development

Code	CONSEQUENCE TARGETS FOR MANAGING PERSONNEL AND STAFF DEVELOPMENT	Does the school regard this target as desirable?	Low priority	Mid priority	High priority
C s 1	Students are well-prepared for life, learning and work	Y			•
C s 2	Students and staff value fairness and reward based on merit				
C s 3	The school community values resolving conflict in the least disruptive way				
C s 4	The staff feel that their career/promotion prospects are enhanced by working at the school				
C s 5	Disruption is avoided and there is consistent continuous teaching				
C s 6	Staff are professionally ambitious and work hard				
C s 7	Teaching is effective				
C s 8	All who work at the school feel that the workload is shared equitably. Effective management is valued by teachers				
C s 9	Deployment of staff is aimed at benefiting pupil achievement				

Target-setting for managing external and customer relations

Research from America suggests that level of parental involvement is related to socio-economic status, and schools that operate in higher socio-economic areas are more encouraging of parental involvement. In fact, heads and principals of schools in low socio-economic areas are frequently found to act as 'buffers' between staff and the perception of negative community influence (Teddlie and Stringfield, 1993).

In the United Kingdom, schools have a statutory responsibility to keep all parents informed and this is largely done through the governors annual report, the school prospectus and newsletters. The parent, as the customer, needs to understand and share the aims of the school. So too does the student who, in many ways, is the customer in the post-compulsory phase. Both have become increasingly assertive and selective in recent times and need to be kept very much up to date if that assertiveness is to have a positive effect on home–school relationships. Consultation needs to happen both for the sake of the customer and for the sake of the organisation.

In many respects, parents are at a disadvantage when it comes to involvement in school affairs – even parents who are members of the governing body. It is in the nature of schooling that they have a limited tenure as customers and can feel disadvantaged by the specialist language used in discussions on curriculum and pedagogy. School managers often do little to remove such obfuscation, failing to realise that an ill-informed parent is seldom a supportive one. The best customer for any business is one that is informed, involved and satisfied.

Parents' obligations to the school are usually set out in home–school agreements. Typically, they must ensure that education is not perceived as something that goes on solely in the school and must accept that, whereas a parent is chiefly concerned with the education of an individual child, the teacher and school manager must view things from the point of view of all pupils.

Generally, research suggests that parental involvement contributes to increased effectiveness (Levine and Lezotte, 1990), but some studies have failed to find a link (Teddlie and Stringfield, 1993). Clearly, the *type* of involvement is important and Reynolds and Teddlie (2000) have identified some typical areas of positive influence: synchronising school and home demands; acting as classroom helpers; fund-raising; helping children with homework; giving feedback to the school or college, and liaising with individual teachers. Research has also shown that:

- In effective schools, teachers are frequently in contact with parents and perceive them to be highly concerned (Teddlie and Stringfield, 1993).
- Effective schools have good communications with parents who form a pro-active partnership with the school (Mortimore *et al.*, 1988; Levine and Lezotte, 1990).
- Effective schools tend to operate an informal open-door policy which encourages parents to get involved (Mortimore *et al.*, 1988).

Table 6.17 Examples of input targets for managing external and customer relations

				Z O N E			
Code	INPUT TARGETS FOR MANAGING EXTERNAL AND CUSTOMER RELATIONS	Yes/No	Historic	Comfort	Challenge	Unlikely
I c 1	Does the school hold parent–teacher meetings at times which are convenient for parents?	N	•			
I c 2	Does the school encourage the involvement of parents in the life of the school?					
I c 3	Does the school have a home–school agreement?					
I c 4	Does the school communicate effectively with the parent body?					
I c 5	Does the school have a complaints procedure for parents?					
I c 6	Does the school have an 'open-door' policy in relation to meeting parents and members of the community?					
I c 7	Does the school interact with the local business community?					
I c 8	Is the school used by community groups?					
I c 9	Does the school interact with other educational institutions?					

Table 6.18 Examples of process targets for managing external and customer relations

Code	PROCESS TARGETS FOR MANAGING EXTERNAL AND CUSTOMER RELATIONS	Target no. of times, % p.a. or amount	ZONE Historic	Comfort	Challenge	Unlikely
P c 1	The school holds .... parent-teacher evenings every ...*(year)*..., from .... to ....for...*(exam)*... year groups	2 1pm–4pm	• •			
P c 2	The school involves parents and governors in some aspects of in-service training and staff development at least..........times p.a. To school facilitates the election of parent representatives and parent governors Senior managers meet elected representatives of the parent body every..........					
P c 3	The home-school agreement is signed upon enrolment and reviewed every.......... by parents and school The school has a homework club for pupils who study better at school in the evening than at home. It is open from..........to .... The school has a home-school liaison officer who visits designated homes on ....occasions every .... A survey of parent satisfaction is conducted every					
P c 4	The school produces a newsletter every.......... The school has open evenings/days every .... The school distributes an introductory video to..........feeder schools and parent groups every .... A survey of parent satisfaction is conducted every					
P c 5	The complaints procedure for parents is distributed at enrolment and reviewed every..........by parents and staff A survey of parent satisfaction is conducted every					
P c 6	Senior school managers and teachers make themselves available on ...., by appointment, for consultation with parents					
P c 7	The school management meets local business leaders and employers every.......... The school has active partnerships with .... businesses A survey of business/employer satisfaction is conducted every					
P c 8	The school is available for use by community groups every					
P c 9	The school has partnerships with ....other schools and colleges					

81

Table 6.19 Examples of output targets for managing external and customer relations

Code	OUTPUT TARGETS FOR MANAGING EXTERNAL AND CUSTOMER RELATIONS	Target no. of times, % p.a. or amount	Historic	Comfort	Challenge	Unlikely
O c 1	..........% of parents attend parent–teacher meetings ....% of parents who attend meet all their child's teachers ....% of parents express themselves satisfied with the timing and organisation of meetings	75% 100% 90%		•		• •
O c 2	..........% of parents attend meetings to elect representatives					
O c 3	..........% of parents express themselves satisfied with home–school liaison ....% of designated homes were visited by the home-school liaison officer on .... occasions. These home visits covered ....% of disruptive pupils The home-school liaison officer meets with external support agencies on ....occasions each year					
O c 4	..........% of parents express themselves satisfied with staff-parent communications More than..........parents attend the open events ....% of feeder schools express themselves satisfied with how and when the school is marketed to their pupils School enrolment is in excess of ....% of the catchment					
O c 5	..........% of parents express themselves satisfied with the complaints procedure The number of complaints per..........is less than..........					
O c 6	..........appointments are made to see staff every term The average length of each appointment is ....% of meetings have the affected student in attendance					
O c 7	..........% of local employers express themselves satisfied with their links with the school ....% of students who leave school for employment, find it with local employers Sponsorship from local business adds ....% to the annual budget					
O c 8	The school sports facilities are available for ....hours each week. The non-sporting facilities are available for ....hours each week The average number of people who use the facilities is ....per ....This is ....% of possible usage					
O c 9	Partnerships with other schools and colleges meet on .... occasions every year					

Table 6.20 Examples of consequence targets for managing external and customer relations

Code	CONSEQUENCE TARGETS FOR MANAGING EXTERNAL AND CUSTOMER RELATIONS	Does the school regard this target as desirable?	Low priority	Mid priority	High priority
C c 1	Education is a partnership between home and school	N	•		
C c 2	Teachers accept that parents have a valuable contribution to make Parents will feel a shared sense of ownership of the school				
C c 3	The school is supportive and responsive to the needs of its students				
C c 4	The parent body is an informed and involved one, supportive of the school and its mission to educate the children of the community				
C c 5	Parents take responsibility for their role in education and schooling				
C c 6	Staff are customer-friendly				
C c 7	The school prepares students for work				
C c 8	The school is part of the community				
C c 9	The school has the mechanisms to learn from other schools and colleges				

Target-setting for managing the built environment

The school or college clearly has an obligation to provide accommodation for its pupils and staff which is suitable, stimulating, safe and properly maintained, although given that more than three-quarters of a typical school budget is taken up with committed pay, improvements to the built environment are usually only cosmetic. Essentially, school buildings should be fit for their intended purpose, include specialist areas and provide a resource for the local community. There should be proper libraries, resource centres, Information Technology (IT) suites and provision for independent study, and outdoor areas should be maintained to a high standard.

Recent advances in Information and Communication Technology (ICT) and its use in teaching has necessitated no small measure of redesign of existing space in schools and colleges, principally in the provision of IT resource centres for both supervised and independent use by students. In some schools and colleges, private finance and finance from official bodies such as the National Grid for Learning, have helped enhance the specialist built environment in this regard. Conversely, the high cost of buildings has meant that schools and colleges are now designed to serve the wider general needs of the community in addition to the specific needs of traditional educational provision. This use of school buildings by the community for cultural, social and sporting activities, increases the occupancy rate and raises revenue for the school, although it does create a tension between specialist and generalist requirements.

Institutions that can reduce their estate costs can enhance efficiency and gain significant competitive advantage (Coleman and Briggs, 2000), but any duplication of facilities – split-site provision, for example – may negate these benefits (Whitehouse and Busher, 1990).

Sometimes, internal school politics can influence the efficiency with which buildings are used for teaching and learning. It is not unknown for subject departments to lay claim to classroom 'territory' on the basis of historical precedent. This is ownership in the worst sense and can make the process of improvement a longer-term prospect than it needs to be.

Research has shown that, in effective schools, learning takes place in a pleasant environment (Creemers, 1994; Sammons, Hillman and Mortimore, 1995) and conditions are conducive to work and study (Rutter *et al.*, 1979; Davies, 1997). So tackling problems such as those outlined above can make a significant difference. The link between the physical fabric of the institution and learning outcomes is fairly well-established (Thomas and Martin, 1996; Bowring-Carr and West-Burnham, 1997), though the impact of the resulting culture on student learning may be indirect at best (Hargeaves, 1997).

Table 6.21 Examples of input targets for managing the built environment

Code	INPUT TARGETS FOR MANAGING THE BUILT ENVIRONMENT	Yes/No	ZONE: Historic	Comfort	Challenge	Unlikely
I b 1	The school has a policy on developing and maintaining a clean, safe and pleasant working environment for its staff and pupils	Y			•	
I b 2	Appropriate resources are set aside annually to develop and maintain the environment					
I b 3	Students and staff are appraised of their responsibilities in relation to maintaining a safe and pleasant environment, with particular regard to litter, theft, lock-up and damage to school property					
I b 4	The school has a policy for visitors and community groups who use the school					
I b 5	The school has a long-term building programme and managers consult stakeholders as widely as possible					
I b 6	The school undertakes to fulfil its obligations in relation to the health and safety of all those who work in the school or visit it					
I b 7	The school maintains proper procedures for first aid, vandalism, theft and break-ins					
I b 8	Specialist equipment is regularly inspected and there is a proper stock-taking system					
I b 9	The school strives to conserve energy within its buildings and staff and pupils are appraised of their responsibilities in this regard					
I b 10	The school regards outdoor play areas and off-campus buildings used regularly by staff and pupils, as part of the built environment for the purposes of health and safety					
I b 11	The school pays particular regard to health and safety at outdoor pursuits centres and for trips away from school premises					

Table 6.22 Examples of process targets for managing the built environment

Code	PROCESS TARGETS FOR MANAGING THE BUILT ENVIRONMENT	Target no. of times, % p.a. or amount	Historic	Comfort	Challenge	Unlikely
P b 1	The environment policy is reviewed every...*(year)...* Minimum standards are set for maintenance, cleaning, safety and staff training. The grounds of the school are maintained to a high standard by the maintenance staff, as are the washing and toilet areas. The school buildings are inspected every...*(week)...*			•	• •	
P b 2	A portion of the school budget is set aside for buildings and the environment, to include maintenance staff costs There are.........members of the maintenance staff (part-time and full-time), totalling .... hours per week Maintenance and cleaning work is inspected every..........by..........					
P b 3	Staff and pupils are informed and reminded of the school's policies on health and safety, energy conservation and first aid at least..........per year. There are litter patrols and safety inspections every..........External doors and windows are checked every..........					
P b 4	Visitors are obliged to check in and out of school buildings. A register is maintained of all visitors to the school, to whom reception staff issue visitor passes. Visitors are invited to comment on the school environment Reception staff receive adequate induction and training The school obtains a copy of insurance cover for community groups that use the school facilities regularly. Community groups are surveyed as to their satisfaction with the facilities					
P b 5	The school estimates future building needs on the basis of enrolment/demographic trends and on the need for renewal. The planning committee meets on at least.......... occasions every..........					
P b 6	The health and safety committee meets on at least..........occasions every year. It meets formally with the senior management team every.......... There is a programme of induction for new staff A record is kept of every accident and hazard					
P b 7	A regular audit is done every.......... on first aid competence among staff. Training is provided whenever necessary A record of breakages, borrowings and theft is maintained First aid stations are inspected and replenished every					
P b 8	A contract is issued each year, by tender, for the inspection of fire extinguishers, fire alarms and intruder alarms. Certificates of compliance are posted in the reception area Safety checks are made on specialist teaching equipment every .... and a thorough stock-take is done every..........					
P b 9	Reminder notices are placed in appropriate places to conserve energy					
P b 10	Safety checks are made, where possible, on off-campus buildings before they are used by pupils. The school maintains a register of recommended off-site buildings and sporting facilities in the area. The register is up-dated every..........					
P b 11	Safety checks are made on outdoor pursuit centres before they are used by pupils. The school maintains a register of recommended outdoor pursuit centres. The register is up-dated every..........					

Table *6.23* Examples of output targets for managing the built environment

Code	OUTPUT TARGETS FOR MANAGING THE BUILT ENVIRONMENT	Target no. of times, % p.a. or amount	ZONE			
			Historic	Comfort	Challenge	Unlikely
O b 1	A total of .... fire extinguishers are installed in classrooms and common areas. There are .... first aid stations in the school Toilet and shower areas are cleaned and disinfected every ...(day)... and checked every ...(day)...	40 8	•	•	• •	
O b 2	..........% of budget is set aside for buildings, maintenance and the environment expenditure on the school environment is £.......... per student There are at least .... hours of cleaning per week					
O b 3	A fire drill is carried out every..........for the whole school The number of false fire alarms set off by pupils is less than..........					
O b 4	..........% of visitors are expected by reception staff ....% of visitors are met at reception by a member of staff ....% of visitors think the school environment good or better ....% of community groups have their own insurance ....% of community groups are satisfied with the facilities					
O b 5	Enrolment forecasts are accurate to within..........% of actual The planning committee produces a report every					
O b 6	The health and safety committee produces a report every ....% of the health and safety committee's recommendations are implemented within .... weeks The induction programme for new staff lasts .... days and is conducted by .... The number of accidents per year is less than					
O b 7	Less than ....% of environment budget is spent on repairing vandalised buildings and equipment Less than ....% of environment budget is spent on replacing stolen equipment At least .... members of staff are competent in first aid. Courses are provided every .... for staff who want to upgrade their skills					
O b 8	At least ....% of fire fighting equipment is deemed fit at the annual inspection Less than ....% of equipment is stolen or damaged every year					
O b 9	..........% of budget is spent on heating and lighting The amount spent on heating and lighting is less than .... per teaching unit and has declined ....% over the previous ...... years					
O b 10	..........% of off-campus buildings used by students are inspected beforehand					
O b 11	..........% of outdoor pursuit centres used by students are inspected beforehand					

Table 6.24 Examples of consequence targets for managing the built environment

Code	CONSEQUENCE TARGETS FOR MANAGING THE BUILT ENVIRONMENT	Does the school regard this target as desirable?	Low priority	Mid priority	High priority
C b 1	Pupils and staff always feel safe. Students associate school with safety and refuge	Y			•
	Ofsted regard the environment as conducive to work and study	Y			•
	Staff feel that the built environment contributed to their teaching success	Y		•	
C b 2	The school is a pleasant environment in which to work				
C b 3	Students learn to take responsibility for their own environment				
	All those who work and study in the school feel a sense of pride in their environment and a shared sense of ownership				
C b 4	The school is safe for pupils but open to the wider community				
C b 5	The school is well-prepared for future developments				
C b 6	The school minimises the risk of accident to pupils and staff				
C b 7	The school minimises expenditure on repairing vandalised buildings or replacing stolen equipment. As the necessity to spend money on repairs due to malicious damage decreases, the school uses those financial resources to good effect in enhancing the quality of teaching and learning				
	Student learn to respect property				
C b 8	Students learn to use modern equipment in a responsible way				
C b 9	Students become environmentally responsible. They leave the school with a raised awareness of the environment and energy conservation issues				
C b 10	Students are comfortable in their learning environment, whether inside or outside school				
C b 11	Students learn the importance of safety in leisure activities				

Target-setting for financial management

The financial management of a school or college is a quantitative exercise and lends itself easily to analysis and target-setting. This is not to undermine its importance. On the contrary, the budget is the means by which the school or college proposes to meet its targets and many schools have a specially designated member of staff (bursar) to oversee it. Moreover, Ofsted inspections look for careful, effective and efficient financial planning, and value for money in terms of educational achievement.

However, using financial analysis to judge effectiveness or 'value for money' is a value-laden exercise and merely reflects priorities determined by the school's ethos. Even management style has an impact on the distribution of resources, as Bush (2000) and others have pointed out (Simkins, 1998), although the dominant style as far as resource management is concerned is clearly a rational one (Levacic, 1995).

Typically, rational management of resources is informed by clear priorities, with spending linked to output, rather than input or process. There is an awareness of the need for planning beyond the usual annual cycle and due consideration is given to alternatives and their spending implications, before the most appropriate choice is selected from the available options. Rational management typically allocates resources, at least in part, by means of a formula that reflects pupil numbers and teaching hours, with an element of weighting to compensate practical subjects for consumable class materials (Thomas and Martin, 1996). It may be incremental or zero-based. 'Incremental' budgeting uses the previous budget as a baseline and adjusts it incrementally to take account of changing circumstances. It avoids conflict and resolves issues quickly. 'Zero-based' or 'needs' budgeting expects internal departments to bid afresh for funding, every cycle. It is time-consuming and disruptive, and better suited to organisations in flux (Bush, 2000).

'Virement' is a partial zero-based budgeting strategy, where managers re-prioritise subject areas and move resources accordingly. It saves time by avoiding wholescale re-invention, but does bring an element of internal competition into the budgeting process.

The practicality of resource management in schools is complicated by the fact that spending takes place over two unsynchronised accounting periods: the financial year (April to March); and the academic year (September to August). Consequently, there is a 5-month period (from April to August) in which staffing costs cannot significantly be altered, though the new budget allocation might demand it.

Income for LEA schools comes largely from two sources: funds delegated by the local education authority through its Local Management of Schools formula, which are linked to enrolment and weighted by age; and funds or surpluses generated by the school itself. The former can range from just over 1000 pounds to over 2000 pounds per Year Seven pupil, depending on the LEA.

Figure 6.5 shows a typical 'income tabulation' for an 11–18 comprehensive school.

Staffing costs – in particular, teaching staff costs – are the largest single item on the corresponding 'expenditure tabulation' (Figure 6.6), typically accounting for more than three-quarters of the budget. Staffing costs rise annually, all other things being equal, with promotions and incremental drift up the Common Pay Scale. There are National Insurance and pension implications associated with all adjustments in salary; and

Item	Amount (£)	Percentage
Reserves carried forward	30,000	0.80%
Income from LEA: age-weighted pupil unit	3,370,639	88.80%
Size related and lump sum funding	339,538	8.90%
Bank interest	6,000	0.16%
Standards fund	13,000	0.35%
Letting and rents	15,000	0.40%
Initial teacher training agreement	15,400	0.40%
Parents Association fundraising	5,500	0.14%
Miscellaneous	2,000	0.05%
Total school income 1999/2000	**3,797,077**	**100%**

Figure 6.5 Sample income tabulation for an 11–18 comprehensive.
Figures based on McAleese (2000).

promotions have the additional real cost of reducing class contact hours for some staff. Consequently, schools now tend towards flatter structures and younger teaching staff, even though staffing costs are relatively inflexible in the short-term (Coleman, Bush and Glover, 1994).

Schools and colleges should make provision for absenteeism and maternity leave as a matter of prudence. Most illness is short-term and self-certified, but some is long-term and the cost of supply cover is significant. Also, the costs of maternity leave are often not fully met by the Statutory Maternity Pay scheme or by insurance and schools should set aside an amount each year, depending on the number and age of female teachers, to make up the shortfall.

Non-staffing costs make up approximately 25 per cent of budget and any savings that can be made in this area will be small compared to those made on staffing. Nevertheless, schools need to consider carefully options like leasing and hire purchase agreements for photocopiers, ICT equipment and the like, rather than outright purchase. Such agreements have the disadvantage of being more expensive, but the advantages of coming with 'free' maintenance and the facility to upgrade equipment every few years at little cost.

The non-staffing budget can therefore be regarded as being in two distinct parts: committed non-pay and non-committed non-pay. The latter is the only part of the expenditure budget which is available for virement, i.e. to prioritise and redistribute among subject areas on an annual basis. How senior managers choose to do this varies from institution to institution, but departmental allocations should:

- reflect pupil numbers or outputs;
- involve a bidding process or be based on historical precedent;
- be weighted according to the nature of the subject.

Item	Amount	Percentage
Administration staff salaries	129,000	3.40%
Technical staff salaries	83,500	2.20%
Teaching staff salaries	2,752,000	72.40%
Supply teacher costs	26,000	0.70%
Lunchtime supervisors	23,700	0.62%
Language assistants	10,500	0.28%
Caretaking staff salaries	40,200	1.10%
Other staff and appointments costs	19,500	0.50%
Total: personnel cost	*3,084,400*	*81.20%*
Maintenance costs: buildings	73,000	1.90%
Maintenance costs: grounds	15,000	0.40%
Electricity, heating, lighting etc	58,000	1.54%
Local authority rates, water, refuse, etc.	125,700	3.30%
School minibus	2,900	0.08%
Furniture and general supplies	20,000	0.53%
Cleaning materials	98,800	2.60%
Total: Built environment	*393,400*	*10.35%*
Administrative materials	38,000	1.00%
Postage, telephones, etc.	11,500	0.30%
Books and classroom materials	114,000	3.00%
Equipment leasing and service	45,500	1.20%
Standards fund expenditure	13,000	0.30%
Quality assurance and ITT costs	13,000	0.30%
Examination fees	68,000	1.80%
Total: Teaching and administration materials	*303,000*	*7.90%*
Grants and bursaries to students	3,000	0.10%
Insurance policies	5,500	0.15%
Health, safety, fire and security measures	5,000	0.15%
Emergency fund	5,000	0.15%
Total: Funding, insurance and misc.	*18,500*	*0.55%*
Total school expenditure 1999/2000	3,799,300	100%

Figure 6.6 Sample expenditure tabulation for an 11–18 comprehensive. Figures based on McAleese (2000).

Finally, it is common practice in some schools and colleges to analyse and present accounts on a per-capita basis. It is a simple manoeuvre to convert Figure 6.5 and Figure 6.6 to per student income and expenditure, respectively, and has the advantage of facilitating comparison across institutions of unequal size.

Table 6.25 Examples of input targets for financial management

Code	INPUT TARGETS FOR FINANCIAL MANAGEMENT	Yes/No	ZONE Historic	Comfort	Challenge	Unlikely
I f 1	Does the senior management team present overall estimates and audited accounts each year which show how the previous year's budget was spent and what is required to improve effectiveness? Does the school aspire to link financial resourcing to increased effectiveness?	Y N N		• •	•	•
I f 2	Does each department within the school prepare budget estimates and accounts? Is the non-committed non-pay budget distributed internally according to an agreed formula?					
I f 3	Are estimates and accounts presented for the curriculum?					
I f 4	Are estimates and accounts presented for staffing and personnel?					
I f 5	Are estimates and accounts presented for buildings and equipment?					
I f 6	Are estimates and accounts presented for home/external matters?					
I f 7	Does the school quality control service providers and contractors?					
I f 8	Is a certain amount of budget earmarked for long-term developments?					

Table 6.26 Examples of process targets for financial management

Code	PROCESS TARGETS FOR FINANCIAL MANAGEMENT	Target no. of times, % p.a. or amount	Historic	Comfort	Challenge	Unlikely
				ZONE		
P f 1	The average income per pupil and the overall spend per pupil is calculated					
	The estimates and accounts are available in...*(April)*...and open to inspection by ...*(anyone)*...upon payment of ...*(5p)*...Priority is given to schemes which have the greatest impact on increasing effectiveness		•	•		
	The manager in charge of financial affairs reports to the senior management team every ...*(month)*...		•			
P f 2	Departmental estimates and accounts are submitted to the senior management team in					
	Training is given to managers with responsibility for financial and resource management					
	The average budget allocation to departments is £..........per pupil, with a weighting of..........for practical subjects					
	An additional sum, not exceeding ....% of budget, is bid for by departments for special requirements					
P f 3	The average spend per pupil is calculated for each curricular area, support services, pre-16, post-16, examinations and INSET and staff development					
P f 4	The average spend per pupil is calculated for teaching staff, management staff, administration staff, maintenance staff, support staff and recruitment costs (part-time and full-time, including national insurance and superannuation)					
	The average spend per pupil is also calculated for sickness, absence and maternity supply cover					
	Provision is made for promotion and performance related pay awards					
P f 5	The average spend per pupil is calculated for building and environment, electricity, heating and lighting, rates, water refuse and sanitation, student travel, furniture and general supplies, cleaning materials, administrative materials, postage and telephone, books, equipment leasing, standards and QA, exam fees, grants, insurance, and health, safety, fire and security measures					
P f 6	The average spend per pupil is calculated for school transport, home-school liaison, disciplinary procedures, advertising and publicity, presentations and communications, and extra-curricular activities					
P f 7	Contract work is awarded by open competitive tender and is inspected by..........					
P f 8	A certain amount of budget, determined after advice from the planning committee, is set aside for long-term development					

Table 6.27 Examples of output targets for financial management

Code	OUTPUT TARGETS FOR FINANCIAL MANAGEMENT	Target no. of times, % p.a. or amount	Historic	Comfort	Challenge	Unlikely
O f 1	Annual expenditure is within..........% of estimate The average income per pupil is £..........and the overall spend per pupil is £..........	1% £2100 £2070	 • 	 •		•
O f 2	Departmental estimates and accounts are accurate to within ....% Training in financial management is given every .... to departmental heads and others					
O f 3	The average internal allocation to departments is £..........per student, which is ....% of the school budget ....% of budget (£) is spent on support services, ...% (£) on examinations, ...% (£) on INSET and staff development, ...% (£) on pre-16 and ....% (£) on post-16					
O f 4	..........% of budget (£) is spent on teaching staff, ...% (£) on management staff, ...% (£) on administration staff, ...% (£) on maintenance staff, ...% (£) on support staff and ....% (£) on recruitment costs The average spend per pupil covering for casual absence is £..........or..........% of budget. The average spend per pupil covering for certified absence is £..........or..........% of budget ....% of budget (£) is set aside for promotion and performance related pay awards					
O f 5	..........% of budget (£) is spent on building and environment, ...% (£) on electricity, heating and lighting, ...% (£) on rates, water refuse and sanitation, ...% (£) on student travel, ...% (£) on furniture and general supplies, ...% (£) on cleaning materials, ...% (£) on administrative materials, ...% (£) on postage and telephone, ...% (£) on books, ...% (£) on equipment leasing, ...% (£) on standards and QA, ...% (£) on exam fees, ...% (£) on grants, ...% (£) on insurance, and ....% (£) on health, safety, fire and security measures					
O f 6	..........% of budget (£) is spent on travel and transport, ...% (£) on home–school liaison, ...% (£) on disciplinary procedures, ...% (£) on advertising and publicity, ...% (£) on presentations and communications and ....% (£) on extra-curricular activities					
O f 7	Work/service is inspected by .... on at least .... occasions and contracts are reviewed every					
O f 8	..........% of budget is set aside for long-term development					

Table 6.28 Examples of consequence targets for financial management

Code	CONSEQUENCE TARGETS FOR FINANCIAL MANAGEMENT	Does the school regard this target as desirable?	Low priority	Mid priority	High priority
C f 1	The school is efficient and effective. It provides value for money	Y			•
	Financial management within the school is open and accountable	N	•		
C f 2	The distribution of funds within the school is perceived to be equitable and encourages departmental and teacher planning				
C f 3	Resources are focused on teaching and learning				
C f 4	Management is focused on the curriculum and staff learn responsibility for planning				
C f 5	The environment is conducive to work and learning				
C f 6	The focus is on the 'customer'				
C f 7	The school expects excellence from its service providers				
C f 8	The school is prepared for future developments				

Summary

- This chapter introduced target-setting tables and benchmarking charts for use in schools and colleges.
- They were based on differentiating between input, process, output and consequence in each of seven major areas:
  - curriculum and teaching
  - discipline
  - leadership
  - staff development
  - external relations
  - the built environment
  - managing finance.
- Each area was discussed from the point of view of school effectiveness research and the charts are based on what that research tells us makes for a successful school.
- A brief discussion on the influence of leadership style and contingency was included, as was a sample income and expenditure tabulation for a typical 11–18 comprehensive school.

7 Introducing and maintaining quality

Having benchmarked internally or against another school and having identified areas for improvement, the question arises as to how to introduce and maintain the new levels of effectiveness and efficiency. Some form of quality assessment and management is required. This penultimate chapter discusses the meaning of quality and how it has changed in recent times, the role of inspection in both output and process, and how to plan for the introduction of quality management systems in schools.

'Quality' can be defined as the objective conformance of output to requirement and is measurable by the extent to which it meets expectations. Of course, for quality management to be successful, client and provider must share a similar understanding of what is expected and in education, this is sometimes problematic. Like commercial organisations, schools and colleges face increasingly demanding consumers whose perception of quality is continually being sharpened by competition. Consequently, quality management should incorporate some ability to change and improve, since it is axiomatic that consumer demands will vary over time. The old common law adage 'caveat emptor' has been replaced by consumer-favoured legislation and pro-choice government, and this is no less true in education than it is in banking or retailing.

Commitment to quality management implies a customer-orientated organisation and should therefore involve a variety of stakeholders. Their coming together will not happen of its own accord. Time, planning and material resources must be provided to support the preparation and training of those involved. Quality is a matter of survival, rather than enhancement.

Quality management by inspection

In industry, quality management was once equated with inspection. Finding and removing sub-standard output was the means of guaranteeing quality to consumers. It was a very expensive and ineffective *modus operandi* and curiously, survives today mainly in education. It was based on the assumption that more inspection meant better quality, but the reality was that quality became a compromise between the ever-increasing cost of inspection and consumer demand for better goods. As frequently happens in such conflicts, an equilibrium was reached between satisfying most customers most of the time, and accepting a certain endemic level of failure.

In education, of course, this principle would only have to be stated for its absurdity to become apparent. Education is a constitutional entitlement and up to 16 years, an obligation. Therefore, there can be no acceptable level of systemic failure. There can be no entitlement to something that does not exist; and there can be no obligation to something that is self-detrimental. The application of traditional industrial-type inspection to education is thus inherently flawed.

In industry, this 'quality by inspection' system changed when choice became a reality for consumers and UK prosperity opened to Japanese trade. Prevention, rather than cure, became the mantra. Quality was no longer perceived as an expensive extra, but as something freely incorporated into the product. The underlying principle was that expensive inspection and rejection was perceived as unnecessary if no substandard work was produced in the first place. Quality became a process issue, not an output issue, and the emphasis changed from quality control to quality assurance.

Today, in education as in commerce, the consumer is even more enfranchised. There is greater choice and schools are more consumer-oriented. Yet the method of inspection has changed little and consequently, neither has the process of quality management. Granted, achieving zero tolerance for sub-standard work is relatively easy in industry, where it can be achieved by limiting variation – the fewer production variables, the fewer rejects. In education, quality management will always have to cater for the diversity in ability that is human nature.

The foundations for successful quality management are well known, whether in commercial or educational organisations. They include good communications, wide staff participation, generic problem-solving ability and effective teamwork. However, traditional hierarchical structures militate against instilling a culture where these features are prominent. School organisations operate in functional compartments within which teachers pursue their own objectives, fulfil their own ambitions and operate to their own agendas. In addition, while teams might operate effectively within each department, an overall organisational coherency is often missing. Variation in one area affects other areas and many aspects of management are 'pareto-efficient' – what one department gains in time and personnel, another must lose (timetabling is a prime example). It is a zero-sum game in miniature. Quality management in education is about getting these balances right, to an acceptable level of tolerance, without reducing creativity.

Quality management by involvement

Already in this book, we have advocated the primacy of process over output. Work should not be compartmentalised to such an extent that the overall sense of mission is lost to all but the senior management team. It should be divided into critical and functional processes, as described in previous chapters, such that an output from one process becomes an input for another. A process sequence is thus set up within and between functional parts of the school. Usually, a process sequence will have a 'terminal output' – an output that does not become an input for another process – and in effective schools, this should be centred on the pupil or parent. The role of quality management in schools is to ensure that each step in the sequence is efficient and effective, and that the fact that teachers usually work in isolation from their colleagues does not adversely affect corporate outcome.

As was mentioned previously in Chapter 2, every critical process should have an internal customer – someone who would buy into a new improved version of a process if one were available. In schools and colleges, internal customers may be teachers, parents, governors or another organisation with professional links to the school. The great strength of the internal customer concept is that it focuses each functionary on satisfying the needs of his or her customer, thereby forcing open channels of communication, which cannot but be good for both the school and the end-user. The facility to take information and give feedback encourages good communication and it is vital that it takes place, whether in formal decision-making meetings or mere dissemination forums. If every faculty and department works in isolation, each will have to develop and duplicate its own response to common difficulties, wasting time and resources, and causing frustration and disenchantment at every turn.

Quality management has its benefits, its shortcomings and its difficulties. In schools, it increases efficiency by reducing wasteful duplication of effort and increases the productivity of teachers by empowering them through the process. It motivates and rewards them with professional satisfaction and competitive advantage. Unfortunately, it sometimes increases stress, particularly among those who are underperforming either through natural ineptitude or circumstance. It increases localised accountability, but demands a considerable commitment from mangers in terms of time and resources.

Inevitably, there will be impediments to progress, not least from the institutional inertia and tradition referred to in Chapter 5. Some are listed below.

- *Lack of planning.* Time and resources should be set aside for early-stage planning. It is not sufficient to simply decide on having a quality assurance system.
- *Lack of commitment on the part of senior managers.* If quality is not perceived as everyone's business, then the school is not ready to proceed. In addition, if quality management is not thought of as a continuous process, then the concept has not been fully understood.
- *Lack of material resources.* Often, initiatives such as this fail through lack of material resources such as secretarial support.
- *Lack of willingness to change.* If necessary, the culture of the school or college must be altered before implementation can take place. Whether this is achieved through inspired 'top-down' leadership or restless 'bottom-up' demand, is a matter for the individual organisation, but a good manager should recognise the potential of dissatisfaction to act as a lever for change.

The need for change

Change is driven by a shortfall between what an organisation aspires to and what it is achieving. There is a performance gap which the school or college hopes to close (see Chapter 4). However, improvement must be measured relative to some baseline and any initial audit of a school or college should include a survey of parent, student and staff perception. This is often overlooked as a starting point for quality management, yet is easily done using questionnaires or semi-structured interviews. The survey instrument can be as simple or as complicated as required, but typically will include a five-point Likert scale from 'Very Poor' through to 'Excellent', and give respondents the opportunity to state both their own perceptions of the school and how they think others perceive it. Experience shows that there is frequently a considerable mismatch between the two! Part of a typical assessment questionnaire is shown on Figure 7.1.

Lack of a clear understanding as to role and responsibility can often be a barrier to quality improvement. All participants in critical and functional processes need to know:

- What output is expected.

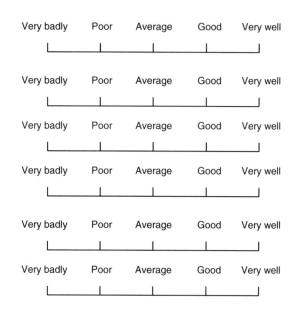

	Very badly	Poor	Average	Good	Very well
How well does the senior management team work together?					
How well does the senior management team work with teachers?					
How well do teachers work within a departmental team?					
How well do teams work across departmental boundaries?					
How well do departments work with individual teachers from outside the department?					
Is there a coherent sense of purpose within the school as a whole?					

Figure 7.1 Sample quality management questionnaire: teamwork.

- The internal customers.
- Whether or not there is an external customer.
- Who is responsible for the processes that provide their inputs.
- What criteria are used to assess quality and effectiveness.

If participants do not know or do not share an understanding of the above, the outcome will either be of reasonable quality, but at a high cost (in time and resources), or of low quality at a reasonable cost.

Wastage

'Wastage' is a difficult concept to transfer from industry to education. Some theorists in industry have proposed that tolerance of waste is a measure of the value of a job (Jaques, 1956), but since teaching by its nature involves duplication of effort – often as an aid to learning – it is difficult to imagine this criterion being applied successfully to schools. Notwithstanding these difficulties, it is possible to arrive at an acceptable definition of wastage that will suit both the setting and the purpose. If quality is defined as the objective conformance of output to requirement, wastage can be defined as its accumulated non-conformance. In education, this can range from deficiencies in sending examination reports home, to duplication of effort in a pastoral care programme. It is potentially so pervasive that its level can only be judged by its effects:

- The number of complaints from parents, pupils and staff.
- Budget overspend.
- More staff doing less work.

- Widespread confusion about individual responsibility.
- Frequent departures from a schedule of planned activities.
- Considerable time spent in remedial measures and corrective action.
- A prevalence of crisis management in the school and a feeling of loss of control.
- High turnover of staff.

Planning to reduce wastage and increase quality

The first step in reducing wastage is to approach middle managers and initiate a quality assessment process. Initially, this will involve proselytising the case for quality assurance, convincing middle managers to convince others and generally enthusing the organisation. Questionnaires will have to be designed and administered, and data collected and analysed. Meetings should be formal, yet friendly, in the manner already described in previous chapters. A discussion of findings from the surveys of perception is likely to elicit conflicting opinions and these will have to be reconciled if the process is not to disintegrate into internecine warfare. The chairperson should be someone capable of tact under pressure. If handled well, the outcome will be a shared recognition of the need for improvement and a growing incredulity that so much wastage was possible in the first place.

Experience has shown that quality management is best initiated by the senior management team, although the need for it should be recognised by all. One of their number should coordinate the planning team and drive the implementation of reform. All the major functions and departments of the school should be represented and a little coercion of those with expertise and influence is not unreasonable. This planning stage is a vital precursor to motivating the entire organisation, since wild enthusiasm often smacks of zealousness and is greeted with cynicism by those who have experience enough to recognise a passing whim. Every '-ism' has its day, but quality management should not be one of them.

Happily, the planning team only has to concern itself with its own organisation, unlike external benchmarking say, although there is no reason why schools cannot learn from what others have done, if they can access the information. The planning team needs to consider the following issues:

- *Aims and objectives.* A mission statement should link quality with expected outcomes for the school. It should be clear, unambiguous and avoid jargonised platitudes. It should define the school's relationships with external bodies, such as parents, governors, local and national government, other organisations (educational or not) and the local community. It should be accompanied by an internal staff memo stating what and how each member of staff is expected to contribute to the objectives, differentiating between output and consequence. Teachers must know what the objectives are before they can share them or contribute to them.
- *Optimal and back-up plans for achieving objectives.* Every plan is contingent on some imponderables and there should be a reserve plan to ensure that the introduction of quality management does not completely stall in the event of a hitch. Both plans should be specific as to how management intends to support the initiative and how school structures are to be geared to that end.

  Quality management procedures do not require alternative structures; that would be counter-productive. The existing school structure – which is what needs to be quality assured – should be used with proper support. One method is to install a 'shadow' structure, so that every department and functional group has a (smaller) mirror image group assessing the quality of its provision.

- *Priorities identified from initial assessment.* This is what grounds the aspiration of quality assurance measures in the reality of practice. The allocation of material resources and time reflects the priority given to different processes, so the quality management budget may have to be front-loaded.

- *Likely objections.* Planners should be sympathetic to recalcitrant staff. Change is unsettling at the best of times and teachers and middle managers need to be reassured that personal criticism forms no part of the process. Quality management is not improvement by humiliation.

- *Dissemination of progress and innovations.* Dissemination needs to be affirmative, supportive and perceived to take account of staff concerns and recommendations. Decisions need to be taken about timing and extent. For example, whether reforms are to be introduced across the entire organisation simultaneously or piecemeal, and whether or not there is to be piloting. Generally, dissemination should find a balance between 'going to press' immediately and perhaps raising hopes unjustifiably, and going too late and losing momentum.

- *How to measure improvement.* This will be the real crux of the process. Some staff will perceive that certain measures favour certain teachers. Some subjects may also be perceived as lending themselves more easily to measurement than others. Therefore, the quality measurement tools used, although they may range widely in sophistication, should all have one thing in common: they should encourage collaboration. Whether the measures of quality are short-term or long-term, methods of measurement, timing and expected output should all be stated in advance, so that the assessment process is perceived as both equitable and realistic.

- *Staff development.* An agreed programme for staff development should be promoted by the planning committee at every opportunity, to reduce any feelings of isolation and siege that may linger in the staffroom. Sometimes, a complete change in school culture will be needed and if this is the case, a more extensive training and education programme will be required.

   If recognising the need for quality assurance is a lever for change, then staff development is its fulcrum. It must be planned carefully to be effective. Different teachers will have different needs and some, like heads of department, will have multiple needs. Some courses will need to be run by external agencies while others will be run better in-house. Realistically, cost will be a factor, but it should not determine the nature of the training.

The process of improvement and reward

There is a tendency in some senior management teams to control the culture of a school by resourcing that which it wishes to succeed and under-resourcing those initiatives to which it is indifferent. However, school improvement research indicates that schools with open communications – where managers give unambiguous direction to staff, take account of the implications of decisions for others and give instructional leadership – tend to have a culture of greater staff involvement and adapt more easily to change. Consequently, teachers and middle managers feel they are listened to and are able to contribute to the overall aims of the school. To change from the former – command and compliance – to the latter – delegation and agreement – requires a *change in* culture, rather than a *changing* culture. Change for the sake of it is not a profitable use of resources. It should be guided by senior managers, who must also take responsibility for improving their own performance. School leadership rather than school management is what is required, so that teachers can give service to the school, made all the more enthusiastic by their own empowerment.

The school's method of promotion and reward will inevitably come under scrutiny as part of the quality assessment exercise, since it relates closely to goal-setting and personal ambition. It hardly needs stating that promotion should be based on merit and perceived to be so, although unfortunately, not every teacher worthy of promotion will receive it. In lieu of it, though a poor surrogate, management should give praise and encouragement freely. Respect from peers is motivating, confidence building and every teacher's entitlement if they are conscientious in the performance of their duties.

Those members of the senior management team charged with implementing quality assurance measures should be careful not to over-bureaucratise the system they introduce. The temptation to replace one set of barriers with others should be resisted. Quality assessment and improvement tools, with appropriate advice on how to use them, should be made freely available within the school, without demarcation, and through training a common language should be developed to enable practitioners to communicate effectively with one another. Everything that is measured should be measured for a reason and should lead to action. Action that is not innovatory should be corrective and it should provoke the continuous cycle of measurement and improvement mentioned at the start of this book.

Critical process diagrams can be used to represent the process in its entirety (see Figure 2.11). If more detailed information is required, it should be represented on process charts like the one on Figure 7.2. 'Suppliers' provide 'input' to a process, which is what is required in order to carry out the process, and an output is the result of it. It is the material or service provided to parents or students, and quality is the extent to which they are satisfied.

Quality measurement should be made against reasonable teacher and student expectation, as indicated by some form of initial assessment and formal examination. If output is not commensurate with reasonable expectation, corrective action of some sort may be required and/or expectations changed (Figure 7.3).

Problems will naturally result from trying to resolve this disparity between expectation and performance. It may be a systemic problem or it may be one of classroom teaching. In either case, the problem may be widespread so certain problem-solving skills should be developed by managers. Brainstorming sessions, where teachers or students throw up ideas as and when they occur to them, is a widely used (though somewhat tired) technique. The ideas are recorded and categorised by the facilitator who orchestrates the session so that it is as inclusive as possible. Ideas beget other ideas. All are noted, none rejected. Simple flow diagrams (like Figure 2.12b or Figure 2.14) or examination matrices (like Figure 7.4) can then be used to try to link cause and effect.

Advanced techniques for recording and analysing measurements of quality are beyond the scope of this book, other than to suggest that any school serious about its quality management should consider training a number of staff in their use. In this way, a team of internal consultants would be readily available to the school.

Range	
From:	
To:	

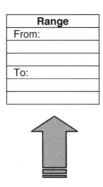

Supplier	Input	Process	Output	Customer

Support required		
Materials	Time	Know-how

Figure 7.2 A process chart.

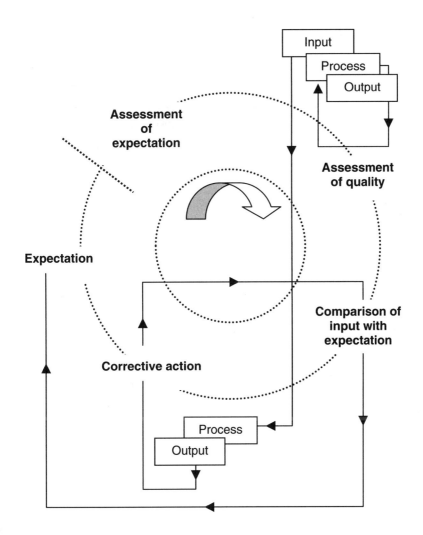

Figure 7.3 Quality measurement and expectation.

Examination matrix

	Task 1	Alternative method	Further queries	Resources
What task is done?				
How is the task performed at present?				
Where is it performed?				
Who performs it?				
Advantages of method				
Disadvantages of method				

Figure 7.4 Examination matrix.

Summary

- Chapter 7 considered the introduction and maintenance of quality assurance systems.
- It defined quality in terms of expectation and discussed the redundancy of traditional methods of inspection and control against a changing educational and economic paradigm.
- The need for change and how to plan a reduction in wastage was presented in terms of commonly occurring issues, including:

  - The need for a statement of purpose
  - Having back-up plans
  - The need for prioritisation
  - The practice of dissemination
  - Measuring improvement and staff development.

8   Networks and communications

Since benchmarking necessarily involves the coming together of individuals or groups of individuals from within an organisation or organisations, the manner in which they form a network is of obvious importance. If, after the benchmarking process has run its course, these partnerships decide on some form of continued relationship, then the way in which the new networked organisation is constructed and understood will determine how useful the relationship will be.

Networks are fashionable. In commercial organisations, their existence reflects the changing nature of the new post-Fordist economic paradigm (Reich, 1987; Reich, 1991); in schools, it reflects an attempt to link improvement to shared and reflective practice. Networks create new types of organisation, for schools as much as for commercial organisations, yet despite this, the intrinsic nature of networking itself and the shifting location of intelligence and value within it are not well understood.

The value in networks

A 'network' is an intermeshed system of information conduits involving individuals or groups of individuals working together towards common goals. The networked system links together factions that have common interests, enabling them to share resources, ideas and experience in an efficient manner. The complexity of networks varies of course, but they all aspire to add value in some way to the service they provide to customers.

'Organisational intelligence' is the ability of the networked organisation to learn and is a measure of its quickness to take meaning from experience. It is the getting and distribution of the knowledge that informs the organisation's purpose. For schools, this largely comprises the collective institutional memory, and the manner in which it arranges itself so as to add value to its service is the key factor in whether or not the network is effective.

There are two features of organisational intelligence, in particular, that make networked organisations different from non-networked ones: where the intelligence (experience and memory) of the network resides; and how the fluidity of its members' efforts affects its effectiveness.

The partition of intelligence in networks

'Network intelligence' is the ability of the network to accumulate, share, adapt and distribute information gained from experience. It imparts value to the actions which the organisation decides to take. The conduits that distribute this information can be 'passive' or 'active'. In other words, they can simply transport information or they can additionally interpret it. Active networks add value because they enhance the passing information.

Where intelligence resides, so too does this ability to add value. If no network exists, then intelligence is static. Value can only be added where it lives. Recently, some writers (Sawhney and Parikh, 2001) have differentiated between 'back-end' and 'front-end' organisational intelligence. The former is intelligence that becomes embedded in the shared infrastructure at the network core. It is centralised, robust and standardised. The latter, on the other hand, fragments into different forms at the periphery of the network. It is decentralised, flexible and contextualised.

The type of intelligence needed by a school at the interface with its students and parents is front-end intelligence, which is very different from the back-end intelligence needed to store and process institutional memory. If more than one kind of intelligence is required at any given place and at any given time, then they may need to be coupled together artificially. What results is a compromise – which does neither justice – between the ability to learn from experience and the necessity to present it in a friendly way to the customer. A school network needs to partition these two intelligences so that the core can efficiently store and process information, while the periphery can be customised to meet the requirements of the individual student or parent, thus avoiding unnecessary duplication.

The partition of intelligence is a determinant of a network's efficiency. In an efficient network, back-end intelligence is not replicated at peripheral points. It is pushed back to the core, where it is embedded in the infrastructure of the network. Meanwhile, front-end intelligence is deliberately fragmented at the periphery of the network, and the conduits between the periphery and the core are hollowed out to become passive, with little or no capacity for generating value (Sawhney and Parikh, 2001). Only the peripheral ends and the core become significant sources of value (Figure 8.1).

The fluidity of effort in networks

The 'effort' of a network is the sum of its individual attempts to achieve its objective, and the fluidity of this effort – how easily it can respond to new organisational demands – is a determinant of the network's effectiveness. It reflects the way an institution organises its staff and its customers, and the way it serves the local community.

In traditional school organisations, individual teachers are tightly grouped in large units of effort, isolated from each other in departments or faculties, like the structure of a solid crystal (Figure 8.2). In contrast, a modern networked organisation, within a school or between schools, has small free-floating units of effort which coalesce into temporary coalitions whenever and wherever they need to, like the molecular structure of a fluid (Figure 8.3).

This notion of fluidity of effort has profound organisational implications. Different individuals or groups can combine their capabilities and resources in temporary and flexible alliances to capitalise on particular opportunities or to address particular needs. Management becomes associated with orchestrating the flow of intelligence and co-ordinating effort, rather than with instructional leadership.

Fluidity of effort requires that a common language be developed within the organisation. Without the existence of a common protocol for exchanging information and experience, individual coalitions could not communicate with each other, never mind collaborate. The clear implication for staff development, particularly in schools, is to develop such a protocol (Figure 8.4).

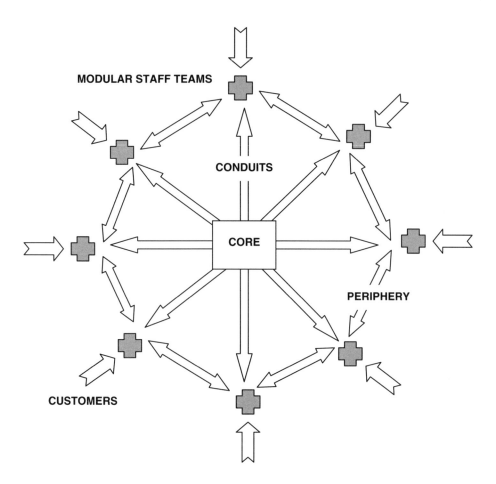

Figure 8.1 A networked organisation.

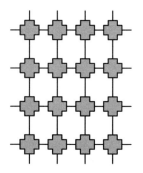

Figure 8.2 Traditional (tightly grouped) organisational structure.

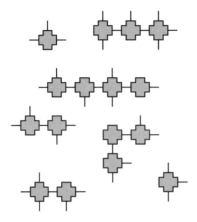

Figure 8.3 Modern (loosely grouped) organisational structure.

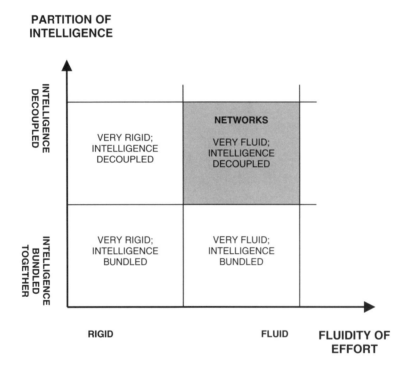

Figure 8.4 The partition of intelligence and fluidity of effort.

The changing location of value

Schools and other organisations preparing for benchmarking or consolidating their relationships in *post facto* networks, must take account of the influence of partition and fluidity on their structures. Modern organisations need to be highly connected to respond to the changed format of information, which is now available in real time, is no longer the province of specialist groups and comes in more user-friendly form. For schools and colleges, the ability to respond to student and parent demands is now more important than the ability simply to teach or do.

The notion of adding value has changed too. In a network, everyone and everything is connected and value behaves differently to a traditional hierarchical organisation:

Value at the ends

Most added value is created at the periphery, near the customer. At the core, generic data-gathering functions consolidate; at the periphery, highly customised connections are made.

Value in a common infrastructure

In a networked organisation, elements of infrastructure that were once distributed among different departmental units are brought together and operate as a singularity. In schools, this shared infrastructure typically takes the form of basic experiential storage functions as well as common business-type functions such as administration, timetabling, marketing and home-school liaison.

Value in modularity

In a network, organisational capabilities and processes are restructured as well-defined, self-contained modules that can quickly and seamlessly connect together. If a value-adding process is defined as a series of modules operating sequentially to create a process by which some piece of intelligence has value added to it, then value lies in creating modules that can be plugged into as many different value-adding processes as possible so that organisational capability can be distributed as broadly as possible (Figure 8.5).

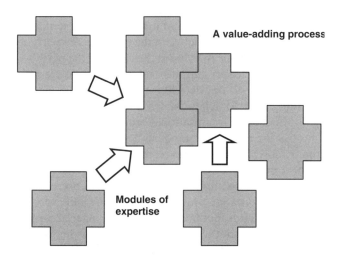

Figure 8.5 The value in modularity: modules that can be plugged into a variety of value-adding processes.

Value in orchestration

As modularisation within organisations becomes more prevalent, the ability to coordinate independent modules becomes a valuable leadership skill. Successful organisations need to be able to develop and maintain their orchestration personnel, over time, for any given value-adding process.

Reshaping an organisation as a network

Partition of intelligence and fluidity of effort are changing the competitive landscape in many sectors, including education. Not surprisingly, the most dramatic effects are being felt in businesses like telecommunications, which by definition are already networked. Traditional telephone companies used to bundle many different kinds of intelligence into their old analog networks. The conduits needed to be active because the simple telephones at the periphery were passive.

The emergence of digital networks made these systems extinct. Intelligence now had to be embedded in software located at the core or at the periphery, so the network conduits could be passive. All that was needed was a fast and reliable link with a little bit of guiding intelligence. Evidence for this shift can be seen in the falling price of long-distance telephony, where the potential to add value is no longer to be had in transporting information around the network, but lies at either end (Sawhney and Parikh, 2001).

The shrinking of middle management in schools is a consequence of this 'pacification' of network conduits as intelligence gets pushed to the core (senior management team) and to the periphery (reception staff and teachers). Networked organisations have less need for middle managers because communication is faster and easier, and collaboration almost unwitting. In old style organisations, before communication became what it is today, there was need for middle management to package and distribute information on its way up or down the organisational structure, between the management core and the periphery. This information-sorting function of middle (departmental) managers has become redundant. Organisations can now have passive pipework, just like telecommunication companies, and the role of middle management, where it exists at all, is to facilitate direct communication between the core and the periphery.

Just as value adding intelligence is now concentrated at the core and the periphery, so too is functionality. In networked schools, leadership and strategic functions are gathered at the core of top management while day-to-day decision-making functions are pushed to the teaching periphery, creating a need for a new professionalism among teachers.

Fluidity of effort is having its effect too. Organisational capability has become more distributed and modular. The passive conduit of modern networks allows dispersed individuals to connect together to solve problems and respond to opportunities as and when they arise. Cooperation between previously unconnected departments is no longer problematic or unusual. In fact, it has almost become an expectation. In schools, parents and students expect access to coherent information from any and every part of the organisation, through web-sites and intranet facilities. It is no longer acceptable to shunt customers from one department to another, claiming lack of jurisdiction. Access to information is becoming increasingly remote and free, and specific interactions between parents and school are more frequently taking place with modular parts of the organisation, rather than with the core.

While such fundamental restructuring of the organisation and the profession within it is threatening, it does offer opportunities.

- Parents and students are better informed and therefore (potentially) more supportive.
- Competing schools can come together more freely to provide better services, safe in the knowledge that engagement and disengagement are easily effected.
- Since communication is efficient and immediate, organisational intelligence can be located anywhere within the network. It can, for example, be moved to a new site to take advantage of expertise or experience, as required.
- A network allows previously unconnected dedicated functional groups to cooperate without the need for restructuring.
- Fluidity avoids duplication, while at the same time assuring quality.

The greatest obstacle to restructuring is a pre-conception of what the result should look like. Reconfigured organisations need retrained managers who have the confidence to overcome these pre-conceptions. Understanding the nature of organisational networks demands that senior managers dedicate resources to the core and to the periphery, to support the value-adding taking place there. Middle managers must change their role from 'filtration' – sorting information as it passes up and down the organisation – to 'facilitation' – orchestrating the interaction between the players at the periphery and the management at the core. Organisational elements at the periphery, where the institution interfaces with the customer, must accept a more responsible and self-directing role, where action is directed by independent judgement and informed by institutional strategy (Figure 8.6).

The challenge for all involved is to prepare the organisation for change; at the core, along the conduits and at the periphery. The following steps offer such a route (Figure 8.7).

- Formulate the school or network mission statement – what the organisation aspires to and believes in.
- Make explicit the policy and aims, which flow as a consequence of the mission statement.
- Elucidate the strategy (or at least an initial strategy) by which the organisation hopes to fulfil its mission.
- Audit the existing structure. Establish the place and nature of the organisation's intelligence and the skills already extant in staff.
- Determine, from the audit, what shortfalls or surpluses exist. Are existing processes adequate? Is the school effectively staffed?
- Examine the location and extent of the value-adding processes. Is back-end and front-end intelligence bundled together unnecessarily? Is the organisational strategy compromised because of duplication?
- Make a conscious strategic decision to centralise core intelligence – intelligence that is shared across constituent operations – and delegate decision-making to the periphery. Decide on the extent of customer access to the core.
- Change from a departmentalised superstructure to a shared modular infrastructure. Consider the notion of fluidity, looking for opportunities to build connections between existing intelligence modules.

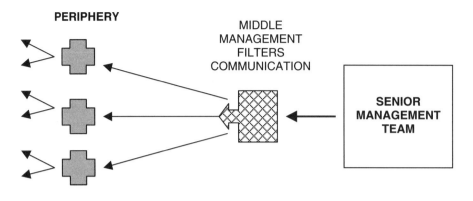

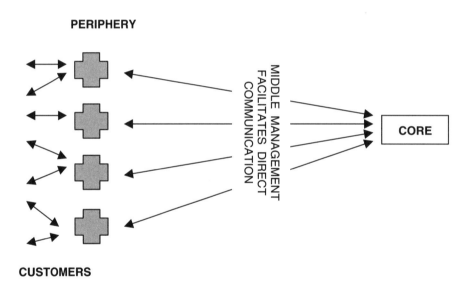

Figure 8.6 Filter and facilitator styles of middle management.

- It is important that every module is, potentially at least, connected to the network. Be aware that isolated parts will undermine the whole. Training should largely concentrate on avoiding this and on developing a shared protocol for internal communication.

A failing organisation is characterised by an inability to adapt, an unwillingness to learn, and inconsistent communications. In schools, this is made manifest by an increased number of complaints from teachers, parents and students; a decision-making process that is perceived as being unresponsive; a growing organisational inflexibility, and a failure to meet the reasonable expectations of staff and customers. Whereas networked organisations are structured to depend on effective communications, poor

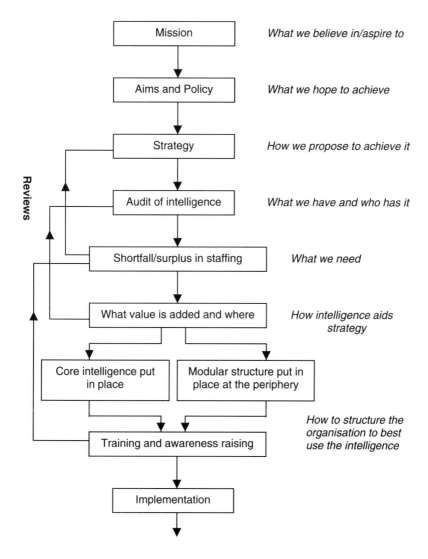

Figure 8.7 Preparing an organisation for change.

organisations build barriers to it. The cyclical flow of information and feedback suffers thrombosis and boundaries grow between hierarchical levels and between subject departments on the same hierarchical level.

Networked organisations are not maintenance-free, however! They may create flatter organisations, but flatter organisations do not remain barrier-free forever. Horizontal (hierarchical) barriers to vertical communication may have been removed, but vertical (specialist-driven) barriers to effective teamworking may remain (Figure 8.8). Network managers must remain vigilant.

Modern organisations equipped to survive and thrive in a networked world are organic and ever in a state of flux. Relationships make and break around issues and opportunities, rather than around competencies or status. The organisation is

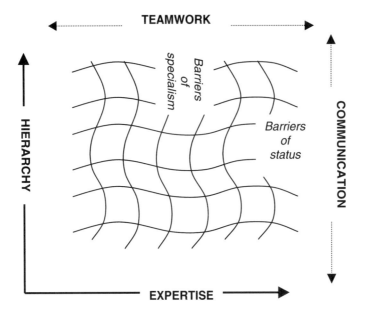

Figure 8.8 Barriers.

characterised by interdependence and reciprocity. Responsibility is devolved among its autonomous modular groups or individuals, who are expected to exercise informed discretion.

Networked organisations adopt a multi-disciplinary approach to problem-solving, achieving outcomes by assembling, disassembling and reassembling coalitions and issue teams (Kelly *et al.*, 2001). They set unambiguous goals and have a shared sense of ownership. Performance appraisal is done in a transparent manner and teams appraise their own performance relative to other teams in the network. Improvement is achieved through the pursuit of exacting standards, supported by a shared sense of responsibility and mission. Consequently, it is in everyone's interest to eliminate boundaries and differentials. Communication between individuals and modular groups, typically focused and direct, takes place irrespective of status, function or location.

Supporting internal and external networking

An organisation's strategic rationale is determined by whether it is driven by internal or external factors. Historically, schools are internally focused and person-driven, concentrating on the human relationships between its internal elements, albeit with some external influence. As a consequence, schools have tended to develop independently of similar organisations, though this situation is changing as more external factors influence what schools do. Networked organisations allow these internal and external influences to interact more freely and allow many and varied connections to be made between an organisation's constituent parts. They allow social and technological processes to interact, whether the organisation is internally or externally networked, while setting a style and culture for improvement.

Internal networking

Internally networked schools have control of their own resources and seek to maximise their use within the organisation by breaking down barriers and creating high-speed quality communication conduits. The creation of specific networks that cut through departmental boundaries also serves to focus expertise and experience around a particular effort, and are therefore usually task-centred.

External networking

The pressure of accountability, the quest for quality and the difficulty of servicing increasingly well-informed customers is forcing school organisations to collaborate with each other, even as they compete. Joint ventures and strategic alliance networks between schools is becoming more common. They are more than remote linkages – they involve a shared control of asset development.

Unlike internally driven organisations, externally driven organisations are not entirely in control of their own development because they lack some vital resource or facility. Networks with other organisations provide that missing resource, but shared control is the price to be paid.

Supporting school networks with Information Technology

Although the investment in infrastructure is usually expensive, Information Technology can be hugely supportive of school networks, whether internal or external, in many different ways:

- An online database allows parents and students to identify and contact relevant people, with a minimum of run-around.
- E-mail allows contact with the school to be immediate and in real time, assuming other forms of communication are impossible or unsuitable.
- Staff communications can be supported by an intranet and students can be given tiered access, if security clearance levels can be arranged.
- Students can use the intranet to track their own progress electronically.
- Administration and financial management can be made more efficient using dedicated software. Quotations, orders, invoices and payments can be made electronically from the core of the network.
- Project teams can work together remotely, especially at the planning stage, through electronic conferencing. Since geographical location is no longer problematic, schools can network outside their catchments.
- Central data storage can be shared within and across institutions, and accessed after office hours, allowing staff to accommodate the many different demands made on their time. Information can be made available on demand, subject to appropriate security restrictions, and staff and students can work from home by linking into the system.
- An electronic bulletin board for staff can encourage shared ownership of information and maintain a sense of institutional identity.
- Remedial teaching can be made available remotely to students who need it. It can be customised and delivered at the most appropriate opportunity.

Supporting soft networks

Staff need to make informal connections with each other, especially in person-centred organisations like schools. A networked organisation can support this by providing staff with 'down-time' and a suitable physical environment in which to share intelligence with colleagues. Soft networking should take place at all levels and cut across both vertical (specialist) and horizontal (hierarchical) barriers. It is not political in the sense of being done for personal advancement, but rather constitutes an alternative informal organisation which allows know-how to be shared.

Admittedly, informal organisations also create alternative power structures. Being 'in the loop' means getting advance warning of important decisions, access to expertise and resources denied others outside the network, and provides a personal facility to pursue opportunity. Soft networking gets things done without having to resort to formal authority. It is based on the expectation of reciprocity – the belief that one will be rewarded for accommodation. It sounds almost sinister, but is really only shifting the nature of the problem-solving game from a competitive one to a cooperative one.

Training and staff development

Traditionally, formal development of staff is primarily aimed at enhancing individual expertise and reinforcing specialism. There is need for this paradigm to shift if the organisation aspires to be a networking one. Expertise is developed anyway through participation in project teams and peer appraisal. It becomes accepted practice that individuals and modular teams keep abreast of advancements in their own specialism without the need for performance-focused staff development programmes. Consequently, personal development programmes need to focus on developing the skills of leadership, problem-solving, communication and participation. As Hastings (1993) says, the nature of an organisation can sometimes run ahead of the ability of individuals to operate within it. People must be given the skills to survive and prosper, including the skill to acquire critical friends to support individual projects.

Individuals and task-centred teams need an understanding of how their organisation functions. This ranges from knowing what resources are available, to what steps must be taken to access them. In particular, staff need front-end intelligence skills – how to deal with customers and stakeholders. They need to understand how networks function, what expectation the organisation has of its employees and who the key people are likely to be in any given situation. They need to be trained in network maintenance – oiling the wheels of information sharing.

Developing staff who can fit into multi-disciplinary project teams is a process that takes time. It depends on individuals having developed a common language protocol and sharing an expectation of excellence, and this must be the priority for all training programmes.

Rewards and incentives

The rewards for a successfully networked organisation include a low turnover of staff and the fact that, when staff do leave – usually for promotion – the organisation has a memory of their experience. Back-end intelligence (know-how and information) is thus retained. Organisations that are not networked, on the other hand, are characterised by partial vacuums, created when leading managers leave for pastures new. They bring the organisation's knowledge with them and the organisation has no memory of what they achieved or how they did it.

Individual staff within a networked organisation benefit too, despite the extra demands made on them. They work in a more satisfying job, they advance personally and professionally, they work flexibly with a wider range of projects and within a greater number of specialisms, they are challenged, their knowledge and emotional intelligence are treated as organisational assets, the process of peer appraisal and improvement creates a learning organisation that develops its own staff, and performance measurement is not feared because the process is supportive rather than critical.

Barriers to networking

Autonomy versus interdependency

Organisations need knowledge workers, to create, refine, adapt and implement innovation. Knowledge workers need autonomy – the freedom to make decisions, the will to do what needs to be done and the ability to improve their own performance. On the other hand, organisations need employees to share information and good practice, and to be able to work constructively with others. This creates a tension that is not always easy to resolve, with the result that the confidence necessary for autonomous endeavour to flourish is not always supported by organisational hierarchy.

Reward and motivation

Traditionally, knowledge workers are driven by the need for recognition, which in the past came from status conferred on the holder by virtue of his or her hierarchical level or specialism. So when status barriers are removed, as they must be in a networked organisation, the reward for knowledge workers disappears with them, and a sense of insecurity replaces it. 'Network status' becomes the new motivation and it becomes a crossweave in the fabric of the organisation. It derives from the individual's connections and his or her ability to open doors for others and to collaborate over a wide spectrum of activities. In a networked organisation, individuals and modular teams are rewarded by being asked to undertake important projects, by being asked for advice and assistance, by being praised in public, by having their work publicised, by being asked to represent the organisation, and by getting more resources and greater remuneration (Hastings, 1993).

The secrecy of expertise

Experts identify strongly with their area of expertise and they gain recognition by visibly demonstrating that expertise to others. Typically, either they hide their professional expertise from outsiders, creating a myth of private knowledge, or they frame the world in terms of what they want to teach, rather than what the customer wants to learn. Either way, an ethos of arrogance removes any obligation the expert may feel to explain to the customer what is afoot and why. This is a barrier to effective networking and is the antithesis of what networking is all about – the ethos of sharing intelligence. Unfortunately, it provides a cultural barrier to change which many organisations find impossible to overcome.

The cult of the maverick innovator

Another barrier to organisational networking lies in the cult of the maverick innovator – the hero seemingly achieving the impossible by himself. Seeking assistance is seen as an admission of failure – of emasculation even – despite the fact that most successful innovators rely on their ability to mobilise other people in pursuit of their objectives, rather than rely solely on their own efforts (Kanter, 1983).

Personal advancement networks

The 'old school tie' network is an organisational barrier to true networking. It occurs when informal soft networks degenerate into personal advancement societies. This, rather than organisational advancement, becomes their purpose. They are typically closed and impenetrable to outsiders and this is what marks them out as barriers. True networks actively seek outsiders and are open, from necessity and inclination.

Refusnik managers

Some managers simply adopt the wrong attitude. They refuse access to information and resources, they refuse reasonable requests simply out of habit, they are too busy to get involved, they suffer from bureaucratic overload, meeting colleagues is a last resort, and so on. Fortunately, organisations are learning how to do without them.

Team networking to solve problems

Networking provides an integrated team approach to solving problems and typically, networked organisations centre project teams around particular tasks.

Multi-disciplinary modular teams

Teams built around issues are constantly evolving and dissolving, as old problems are solved and new ones present themselves. Although these multi-functional and multi-disciplinary teams are the result of a networking culture, the network is, in many ways, the product of the belief that improvement itself can be viewed as an infinite series of incremental steps.

A modular team will sometimes be visible and formally instituted. At other times, it will be invisible and have a very short life span. Which it is, depends largely on the nature of the issue around which the group is gathered and its success or failure depends on the extent to which its members share an understanding of the fundamental nature of the problem under consideration, assuming that it is adequately resourced and given a long enough time scale.

A team's mix of expertise and experience, rather than the status of its members, is also crucial to its success. Individuals should belong to it because they can contribute to its success, not because they enhance its status, so quality moderation within the team is not a hierarchical function, but peer-imposed. Members are driven by the status of success and the need for achievement. Their reward is the status they get out of it, not the status they bring to it. They have the privilege of autonomy, but they also carry the burden of accountability and the pressure to perform for the common good, which is a common feature of all successful teams.

Suitability of some tasks to a team approach

Of course, not every task in a networked organisation needs to be tackled by modular teams. There is still room for traditional, hierarchical line management and it would be as silly to complicate matters unnecessarily as to over-simplify them. Teams work better in some areas than others.

Obviously, anything that requires cross-functional thinking or inter-departmental contact is more suited to teamwork than individual endeavour. Restructuring strategic processes and issues relating to staff development are also team pursuits. They are the ones which shape the future for the organisation and are by their nature, complicated. Modular teams dealing with these issues usually require a certain minimum threshold of experience and expertise, and an ability to achieve consensus within the team.

Problems associated with team working

There are real problems associated with team working:

- Teams may fail because management has failed to support them. Team members can overcome this problem by canvassing support from critical friends. The project may need 'sponsorship' from a senior manager.
- Individual expectation may not be matched by that of the collective and the team may find it impossible to agree priorities.
- Teams may find it difficult to meet in person because of geographical separation and communication may have to be electronic. This is usually adequate for basic information transfer, but it fails to build cohesiveness or a shared sense of purpose. Members forget that they are members of a team (Hastings, 1993). Putting a multi-disciplinary group of individuals together and giving them a task does not in itself create a team. Communication problems inhibit a team's ability to morph into a high-performance entity (and cultural factors may exaggerate them) so teams must first build a common language protocol.
- The team may have members who can contribute to the successful accomplishment of the task, but who may be opinionated individualists with a desire for autonomy that outweighs their desire to contribute to the collective.
- Even when teams do come together, meetings may be badly managed and generally unproductive. Staff need training in these management skills and they need to be given the opportunity to practise them.
- Teams may become self-justifying and neglect their duty to relate to the rest of the organisation. Lack of hierarchy may actually compound this problem, as the formal links within the home organisation may have disappeared.

Managing a network of projects

An organisation with an ever-changing mix of task-centred project groups, involving different combinations of people at different times, presents senior managers with new challenges in tracking, prioritisation and monitoring. They must, for example, keep track of all the projects-in-progress at any one time – what Hastings (1993) calls the 'portfolio' of organisational work. It can be managed by ensuring that output is linked to strategy and that defunct projects are shut down and staffing reconfigured among 'live' groups. Senior management is also responsible for creating a 'learning to learn' ethos within the organisation, which aims to increase the organisation's collective experience after every project (Hargreaves, 1997; Argyris, 1999).

However, putting people together and getting the right mix is something that comes from both management and staff. A networked organisation demands that its staff take responsibility, rather than merely accepting instruction.

Sharing conscious expertise

Expertise is not solely about knowledge and information. It is about experience and the skill of being able to marry know-how with know-why. When individuals or teams of individuals leave an organisation, the organisation must retain a copy of their expertise, although of course the 'original' leaves with them. Unlike traditional hierarchical structures, networks are ideal structures to do this. The core intelligence – the organisational memory – stores it, but for it to be useful in the future, it must be transferable to different locations throughout the network.

Staff move this stored expertise from the core to the periphery, so network management is primarily concerned with developing 'conscious expertise' among its employees – know-how that the holders know they know. Put another way, it is important for an organisation to know what it does not know. Conscious expertise is superior to the subconscious sort, since it allows the doer to replicate what is effective. As organisations modernise, they must, in part at least, learn how to use it to enhance performance.

The key to successful transferability is that whatever is to be transferred resides in the network in a format which the common protocol can access. The need for developing such a protocol has been mentioned already. It allows for effective communication and the efficient diffusion of know-how to take place, though the way in which project teams access diffusing expertise within the organisation is limited by the nature of the expertise and the personal skills of those who have access to it.

The way in which individuals and teams 'bank' their expertise at the core, for distribution to others around the network, reflects their perception of their own expertise. For instance, they may well not value a particular skill, even though it is sorely needed by others in another location. Therefore, it is important for employees to know what they know and to value what they know. Let the usefulness of expertise be judged on its use by others, not prejudiced by the value its owner puts on it.

Full surrender of expertise to the network allows the core intelligence to identify who in the organisation has the required expertise to work on particular problems. Effective teams can be put together with this information, tailored to the task at hand, bringing together the right people in the right proportions at the right time. That is the fundamental purpose of network management; to bring surrender of information to storage and back to the periphery again.

Summary

- This final chapter considered the concepts that underpin networking in organisations: fluidity of effort and the partition of value-adding organisational intelligence.
- It discussed how the nature of organisations has changed in recent times to reflect the changing nature of communication and customer expectation, and how value is now created only at the core and at the periphery, not in the conduits themselves.

- It discussed the process of reshaping organisations as networks, the challenges for management in doing so, the structures that can be used to support networking and the barriers that typically undermine it.
- Finally, the use and nature of teamworking was considered, along with motivation and the importance of sharing conscious expertise.

Conclusion

Benchmarking is a journey, not a destination. For schools, it is a journey over the uncertain terrain of school effectiveness, between two places that differ only in the extent to which they are regarded as successful. Quality assurance procedures provide a map for that journey, pinpointing location and indicating direction.

The search for responsive democratic institutions is part of this odyssey. The vehicle of choice is an effective networked organisation and the planned destination is an improved service for customers.

Supporting quality assurance and networking structures is a considerable organisational commitment. The end of the industrial economy and the effect of this on organisations mean that traditional methods of inspection and control no longer work. Gone too are the managerial gatekeepers; those who would manage the flow of intelligence between parts of the structure. Empowerment and responsibility is the new order and it requires a new breed of collaborative manager to succeed against this ever-changing landscape. They need to exercise leadership rather than command. They must imbue their organisations with vision and their employees with enthusiasm. Above all, they must embrace change and rise to the challenge of knowing how to harness it.

Appendix

Benchmarking comparison charts

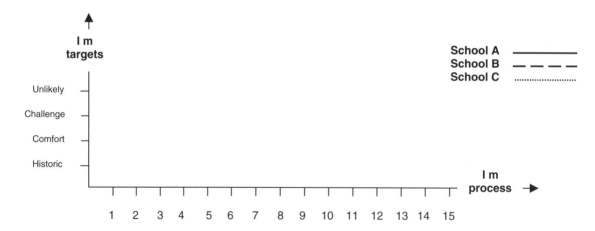

Code	School A					School B					School C			
	Historic	Comfort	Challenge	Unlikely		Historic	Comfort	Challenge	Unlikely		Historic	Comfort	Challenge	Unlikely
I m 1														
I m 2														
I m 3														
I m 4														
I m 5														
I m 6														
I m 7														
I m 8														
I m 9														
I m 10														
I m 11														
I m 12														
I m 13														
I m 14														
I m 15														

School A ——————
School B — — — —
School C ·················

I m targets

Unlikely —
Challenge —
Comfort —
Historic —

I m process →

1 2 3 4 5 6 7 8 9 10 11 12 13 14 15

Chart 1 Comparison chart for input targets: teaching and managing the curriculum.

126

Code	Historic	Comfort	Challenge	Unlikely		Historic	Comfort	Challenge	Unlikely		Historic	Comfort	Challenge	Unlikely
I t 1														
I t 2														
I t 3														
I t 4														
I t 5														
I t 6														
I t 7														
I t 8														
I t 9														
I t 10														
I t 11														
I t 12														
I t 13														
I t 14														
I t 15														

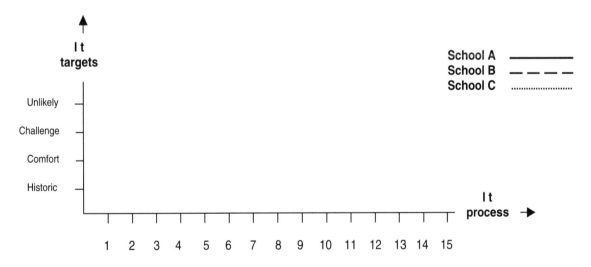

I t
targets

School A ————
School B — — — —
School C ·············

Unlikely

Challenge

Comfort

Historic

I t
process →

1 2 3 4 5 6 7 8 9 10 11 12 13 14 15

Chart 1 (cont.).

Code	School A						School B						School C				
	Target no. of times, % p.a. or amount	Historic	Comfort	Challenge	Unlikely		Target no. of times, % p.a. or amount	Historic	Comfort	Challenge	Unlikely		Target no. of times, % p.a. or amount	Historic	Comfort	Challenge	Unlikely
P m 1																	
P m 2																	
P m 3																	
P m 4																	
P m 5																	
P m 6																	
P m 7	/																
P m 8																	
P m 9	/																
P m 10																	
P m 11																	
P m 12																	
P m 13																	
P m 14																	
P m 15																	

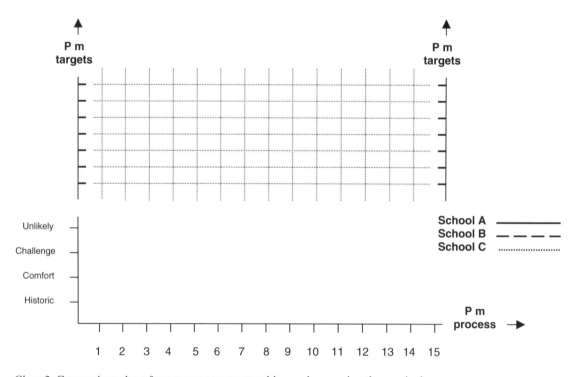

P m
targets

P m
targets

Unlikely

Challenge

Comfort

Historic

School A ——————
School B — — — —
School C ·················

P m
process →

1 2 3 4 5 6 7 8 9 10 11 12 13 14 15

Chart 2 Comparison chart for process targets: teaching and managing the curriculum.

128

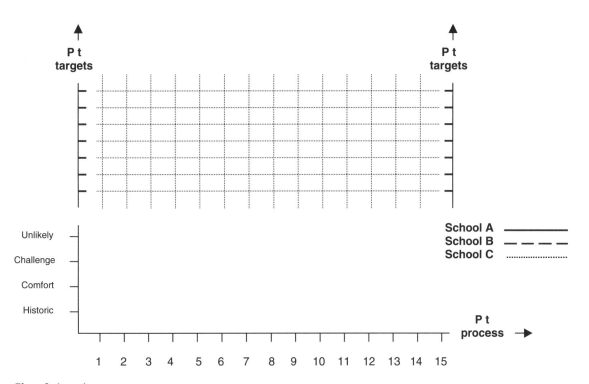

Code	Target no. of times, % p.a. or amount	Historic	Comfort	Challenge	Unlikely		Target no. of times, % p.a. or amount	Historic	Comfort	Challenge	Unlikely		Target no. of times, % p.a. or amount	Historic	Comfort	Challenge	Unlikely
P t 1																	
P t 2																	
P t 3																	
P t 4																	
P t 5																	
P t 6																	
P t 7	/																
P t 8																	
P t 9																	
P t 10																	
P t 11	/																
P t 12																	
P t 13																	
P t 14																	
P t 15																	

P t targets

P t targets

Unlikely —
Challenge —
Comfort —
Historic —

School A ————
School B — — — —
School C ....

P t process →

1 2 3 4 5 6 7 8 9 10 11 12 13 14 15

Chart 2 (cont.).

Code	School A						School B						School C				
	Target no. of times, % p.a. or amount	Historic	Comfort	Challenge	Unlikely		Target no. of times, % p.a. or amount	Historic	Comfort	Challenge	Unlikely		Target no. of times, % p.a. or amount	Historic	Comfort	Challenge	Unlikely
O m 1																	
O m 2	/																
O m 3	/																
O m 4	/																
O m 5																	
O m 6	/																
O m 7	/																
O m 8																	
O m 9																	
O m 10																	
O m 11																	
O m 12	/ / / /																
O m 13																	
O m 14	/																
O m 15	/																

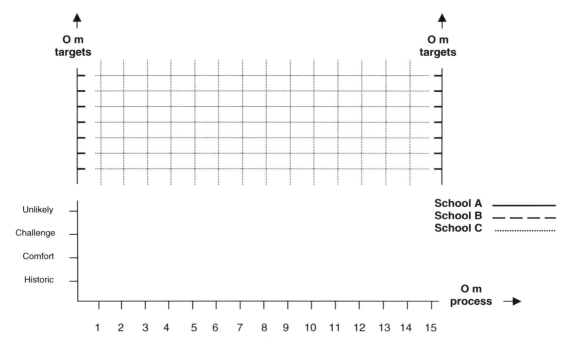

School A ———
School B — — — —
School C ....

Chart 3 Comparison chart for output targets: teaching and managing the curriculum.

130

Code	Target no. of times, % p.a. or amount	Historic	Comfort	Challenge	Unlikely	Target no. of times, % p.a. or amount	Historic	Comfort	Challenge	Unlikely	Target no. of times, % p.a. or amount	Historic	Comfort	Challenge	Unlikely
O t 1															
O t 2															
O t 3	/														
O t 4															
O t 5															
O t 6															
O t 7	/ / /														
O t 8	/														
O t 9															
O t 10	/														
O t 11															
O t 12	/														
O t 13															
O t 14	/														
O t 15															

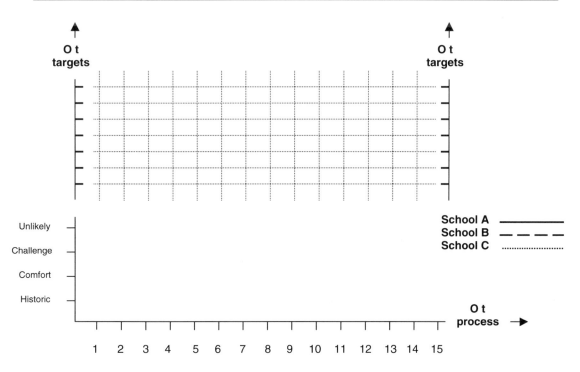

O t targets

O t targets

Unlikely
Challenge
Comfort
Historic

School A ——————
School B – – – – –
School C ·····················

O t process →

1 2 3 4 5 6 7 8 9 10 11 12 13 14 15

Chart 3 (cont.).

Code	School A					School B					School C			
	To what extent (0–100%) is this outcome achieved?	Low priority	Mid priority	High priority		To what extent (0–100%) is this outcome achieved?	Low priority	Mid priority	High priority		To what extent (0–100%) is this outcome achieved?	Low priority	Mid priority	High priority
C m 1														
C m 2														
C m 3														
C m 4														
C m 5														
C m 6														
C m 7														
C m 8														
C m 9														
C m 10														
C m 11														
C m 12														
C m 13														
C m 14														
C m 15														

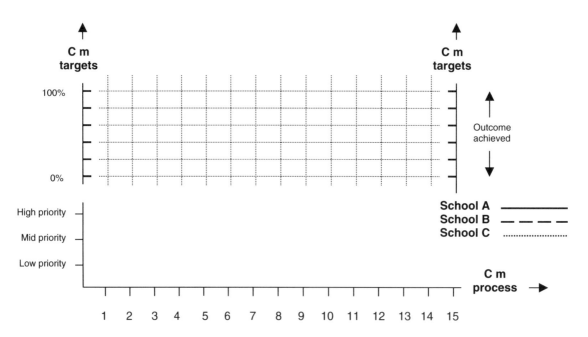

Chart 4 Comparison chart for consequence targets: teaching and managing the curriculum.

Code	School A					School B					School C			
	To what extent (0–100%) is this outcome achieved?	Low priority	Mid priority	High priority		To what extent (0–100%) is this outcome achieved?	Low priority	Mid priority	High priority		To what extent (0–100%) is this outcome achieved?	Low priority	Mid priority	High priority
C t 1														
C t 2														
C t 3														
C t 4														
C t 5														
C t 6														
C t 7														
C t 8														
C t 9														
C t 10														
C t 11														
C t 12														
C t 13														
C t 14														
C t 15														

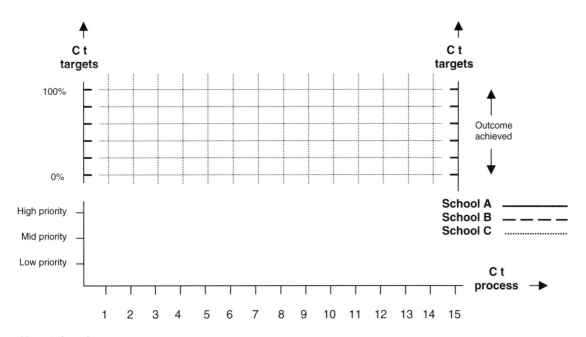

Chart 4 (cont.).

Code	School A					School B					School C			
	Historic	Comfort	Challenge	Unlikely		Historic	Comfort	Challenge	Unlikely		Historic	Comfort	Challenge	Unlikely
Id 1														
Id 2														
Id 3														
Id 4														
Id 5														
Id 6														
Id 7														
Id 8														
Id 9														
Id 10														
Id 11														

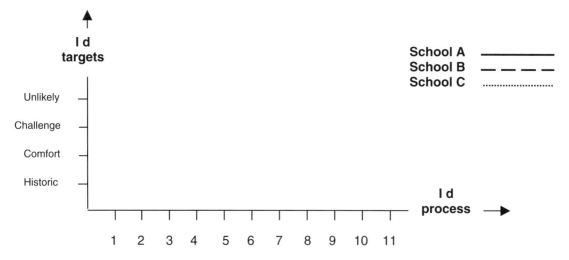

Chart 5 Comparison chart for input targets: discipline.

Code	School A						School B						School C				
	Target no. of times, % p.a. or amount	Historic	Comfort	Challenge	Unlikely		Target no. of times, % p.a. or amount	Historic	Comfort	Challenge	Unlikely		Target no. of times, % p.a. or amount	Historic	Comfort	Challenge	Unlikely
P d 1	/ /																
P d 2	/																
P d 3	/																
P d 4	/																
P d 5																	
P d 6																	
P d 7																	
P d 8	/																
P d 9	/																
P d 10																	
P d 11																	

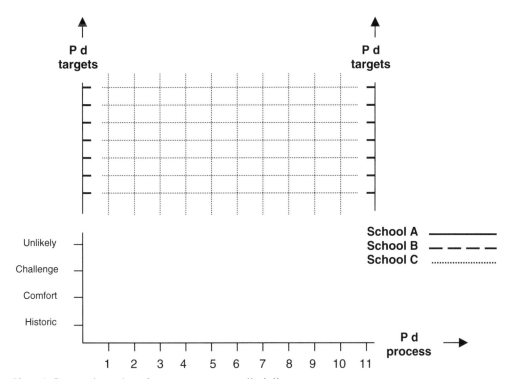

Chart 6 Comparison chart for process targets: discipline.

135

Code	School A						School B						School C				
	Target no. of times, % p.a. or amount	Historic	Comfort	Challenge	Unlikely		Target no. of times, % p.a. or amount	Historic	Comfort	Challenge	Unlikely		Target no. of times, % p.a. or amount	Historic	Comfort	Challenge	Unlikely
O d 1	/ / /																
O d 2																	
O d 3	/																
O d 4																	
O d 5																	
O d 6	/																
O d 7	/																
O d 8																	
O d 9	/																
O d 10																	
O d 11	/																

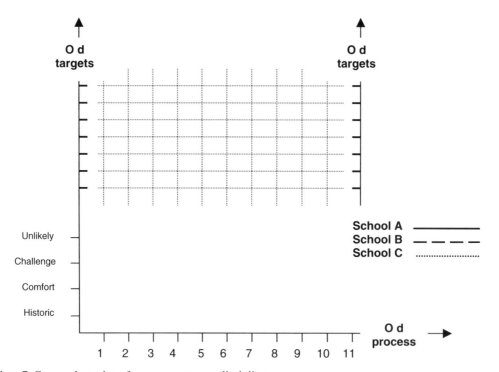

Chart 7 Comparison chart for output targets: discipline.

Code	School A					School B					School C			
	To what extent is this outcome achieved? (0–100%)	Low priority	Mid priority	High priority		To what extent is this outcome achieved? (0–100%)	Low priority	Mid priority	High priority		To what extent is this outcome achieved? (0–100%)	Low priority	Mid priority	High priority
C d 1														
C d 2														
C d 3														
C d 4														
C d 5														
C d 6														
C d 7														
C d 8														
C d 9														
C d 10														
C d 11														

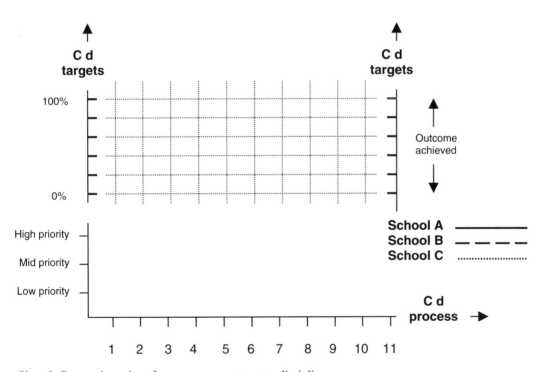

Chart 8 Comparison chart for consequence targets: discipline.

Code	School A					School B					School C			
	Historic	Comfort	Challenge	Unlikely		Historic	Comfort	Challenge	Unlikely		Historic	Comfort	Challenge	Unlikely
I L 1														
I L 2														
I L 3														
I L 4														
I L 5														
I L 6														
I L 7														
I L 8														
I L 9														
I L 10														
I L 11														

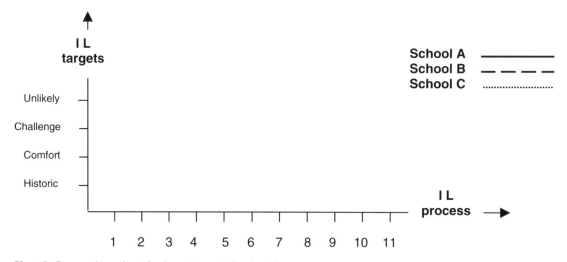

Chart 9 Comparison chart for input targets: leadership.

Code	School A						School B						School C					
	Target no. of times, % p.a. or amount	Historic	Comfort	Challenge	Unlikely		Target no. of times, % p.a. or amount	Historic	Comfort	Challenge	Unlikely		Target no. of times, % p.a. or amount	Historic	Comfort	Challenge	Unlikely	
P L 1	/																	
P L 2	/																	
P L 3	/																	
P L 4	/																	
P L 5	/																	
P L 6	/																	
P L 7																		
P L 8	/																	
P L 9	/																	
P L 10																		
P L 11																		

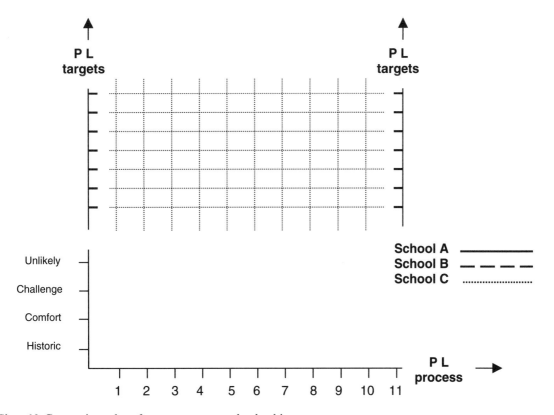

PL targets   PL targets

School A —————
School B — — — —
School C ·················

Unlikely

Challenge

Comfort

Historic

1   2   3   4   5   6   7   8   9   10   11

PL process

Chart 10 Comparison chart for process targets: leadership.

Code	School A						School B						School C				
	Target no. of times, % p.a. or amount	Historic	Comfort	Challenge	Unlikely		Target no. of times, % p.a. or amount	Historic	Comfort	Challenge	Unlikely		Target no. of times, % p.a. or amount	Historic	Comfort	Challenge	Unlikely
O L 1	/																
O L 2	/																
O L 3	/																
O L 4																	
O L 5	/																
O L 6	/																
O L 7	/																
O L 8	/																
O L 9	/																
O L 10																	
O L 11	/																

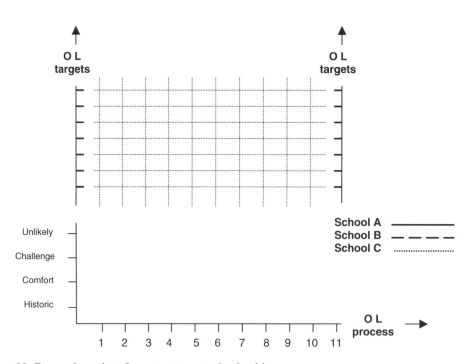

Chart 11 Comparison chart for output targets: leadership.

140

Code	School A					School B					School C			
	To what extent (0–100%) is this outcome achieved?	Low priority	Mid priority	High priority		To what extent (0–100%) is this outcome achieved?	Low priority	Mid priority	High priority		To what extent (0–100%) is this outcome achieved?	Low priority	Mid priority	High priority
C L 1														
C L 2														
C L 3														
C L 4														
C L 5														
C L 6														
C L 7														
C L 8														
C L 9														
C L 10														
C L 11														

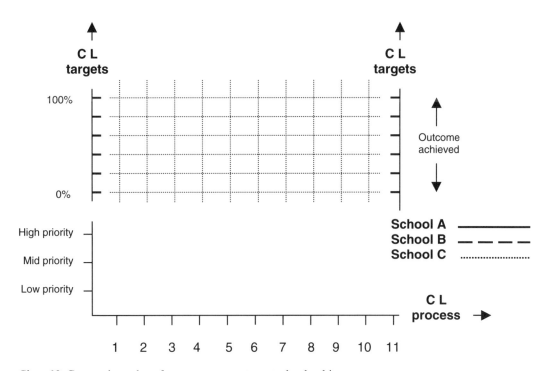

Chart 12 Comparison chart for consequence targets: leadership.

141

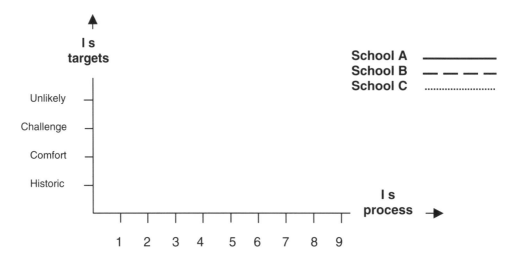

Code	School A					School B					School C			
	Historic	Comfort	Challenge	Unlikely		Historic	Comfort	Challenge	Unlikely		Historic	Comfort	Challenge	Unlikely
I s 1														
I s 2														
I s 3														
I s 4														
I s 5														
I s 6														
I s 7														
I s 8														
I s 9														

Chart 13 Comparison chart for input targets: managing personnel and staff development.

Code	School A							School B							School C					
	Target no. of times, % p.a. or amount	Historic	Comfort	Challenge	Unlikely			Target no. of times, % p.a. or amount	Historic	Comfort	Challenge	Unlikely			Target no. of times, % p.a. or amount	Historic	Comfort	Challenge	Unlikely		
P s 1																					
P s 2	/																				
P s 3																					
P s 4																					
P s 5																					
P s 6																					
P s 7																					
P s 8																					
P s 9																					

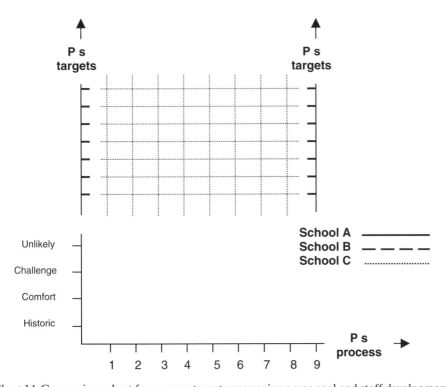

School A ——————
School B — — — —
School C ....

Chart 14 Comparison chart for process targets: managing personnel and staff development.

Code	School A						School B						School C				
	Target no. of times, % p.a. or amount	Historic	Comfort	Challenge	Unlikely		Target no. of times, % p.a. or amount	Historic	Comfort	Challenge	Unlikely		Target no. of times, % p.a. or amount	Historic	Comfort	Challenge	Unlikely
O s 1	/																
O s 2	/																
O s 3	/																
O s 4	/ /																
O s 5	/																
O s 6																	
O s 7																	
O s 8	/ / /																
O s 9	/																

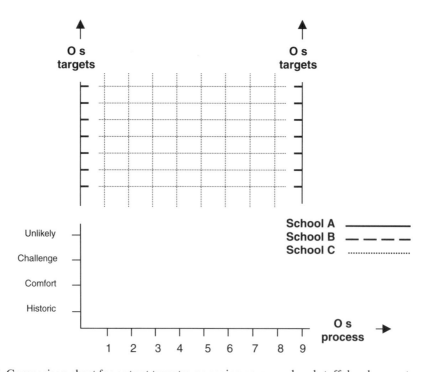

O s targets

O s targets

Unlikely
Challenge
Comfort
Historic

School A ——————
School B — — — —
School C ....

1 2 3 4 5 6 7 8 9

O s process

Chart 15 Comparison chart for output targets: managing personnel and staff development.

Code	School A					School B					School C			
	To what extent (0–100%) is this outcome achieved?	Low priority	Mid priority	High priority		To what extent (0–100%) is this outcome achieved?	Low priority	Mid priority	High priority		To what extent (0–100%) is this outcome achieved?	Low priority	Mid priority	High priority
C s 1														
C s 2														
C s 3														
C s 4														
C s 5														
C s 6														
C s 7														
C s 8														
C s 9														

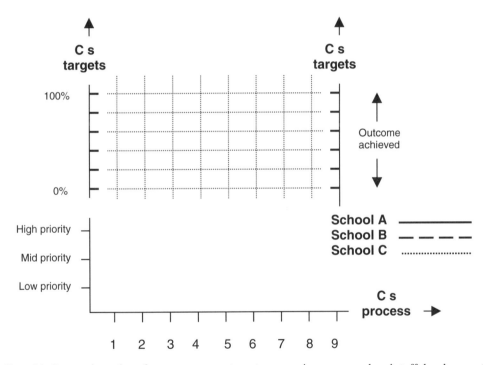

Chart 16 Comparison chart for consequence targets: managing personnel and staff development.

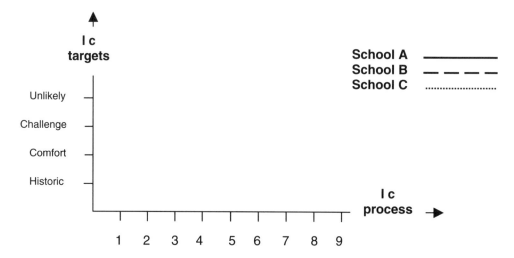

Code	School A					School B					School C			
	Historic	Comfort	Challenge	Unlikely		Historic	Comfort	Challenge	Unlikely		Historic	Comfort	Challenge	Unlikely
I c 1														
I c 2														
I c 3														
I c 4														
I c 5														
I c 6														
I c 7														
I c 8														
I c 9														

Chart 17 Comparison chart for input targets: managing external and customer relations.

Code	School A							School B							School C					
	Target no. of times, % p.a. or amount	Historic	Comfort	Challenge	Unlikely			Target no. of times, % p.a. or amount	Historic	Comfort	Challenge	Unlikely			Target no. of times, % p.a. or amount	Historic	Comfort	Challenge	Unlikely		
P c 1	/ /																				
P c 2																					
P c 3	/ /																				
P c 4	/																				
P c 5																					
P c 6																					
P c 7																					
P c 8																					
P c 9																					

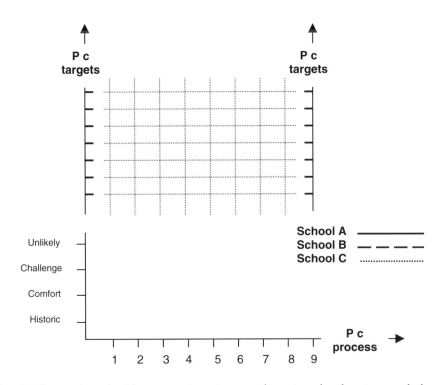

Chart 18 Comparison chart for process targets: managing external and customer relations.

Code	School A						School B						School C				
	Target no. of times, % p.a. or amount	Historic	Comfort	Challenge	Unlikely		Target no. of times, % p.a. or amount	Historic	Comfort	Challenge	Unlikely		Target no. of times, % p.a. or amount	Historic	Comfort	Challenge	Unlikely
O c 1																	
O c 2																	
O c 3		/															
O c 4																	
O c 5		/															
O c 6																	
O c 7																	
O c 8		/															
O c 9																	

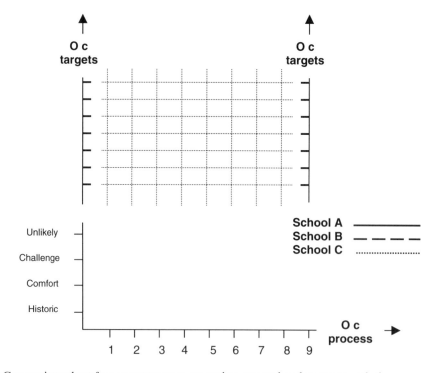

O c targets   O c targets

Unlikely
Challenge
Comfort
Historic

School A ————
School B — — — —
School C ················

1 2 3 4 5 6 7 8 9

O c process

Chart 19 Comparison chart for output targets: managing external and customer relations.

148

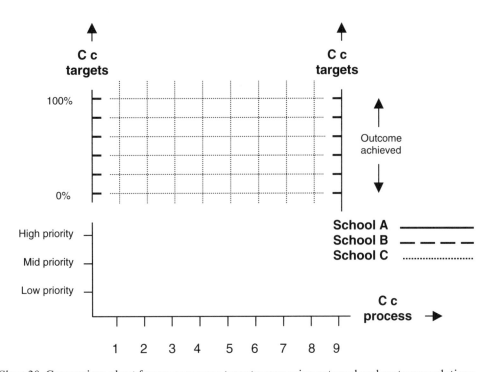

Code	School A					School B					School C			
	To what extent (0–100%) is this outcome achieved?	Low priority	Mid priority	High priority		To what extent (0–100%) is this outcome achieved?	Low priority	Mid priority	High priority		To what extent (0–100%) is this outcome achieved?	Low priority	Mid priority	High priority
C c 1														
C c 2														
C c 3														
C c 4														
C c 5														
C c 6														
C c 7														
C c 8														
C c 9														

Chart 20 Comparison chart for consequence targets: managing external and customer relations.

Code	School A					School B					School C			
	Historic	Comfort	Challenge	Unlikely		Historic	Comfort	Challenge	Unlikely		Historic	Comfort	Challenge	Unlikely
I b 1														
I b 2														
I b 3														
I b 4														
I b 5														
I b 6														
I b 7														
I b 8														
I b 9														
I b 10														
I b 11														

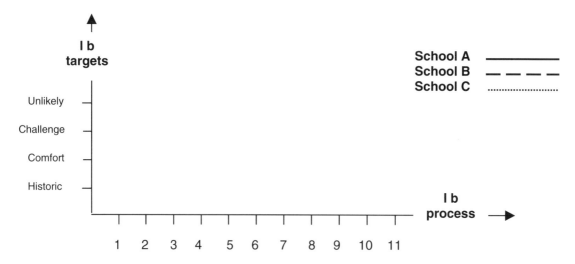

I b targets

Unlikely
Challenge
Comfort
Historic

School A ———
School B — — —
School C ·········

1 2 3 4 5 6 7 8 9 10 11

I b process →

Chart 21 Comparison chart for input targets: managing the built environment.

Code	School A						School B						School C				
	Target no. of times, % p.a. or amount	Historic	Comfort	Challenge	Unlikely		Target no. of times, % p.a. or amount	Historic	Comfort	Challenge	Unlikely		Target no. of times, % p.a. or amount	Historic	Comfort	Challenge	Unlikely
P b 1																	
P b 2	/ /																
P b 3																	
P b 4																	
P b 5	/																
P b 6																	
P b 7																	
P b 8	/																
P b 9																	
P b 10																	
P b 11																	

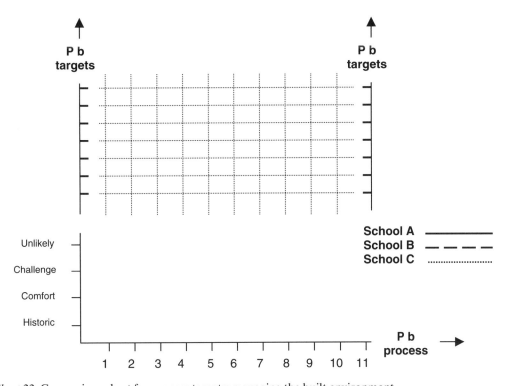

School A ———————
School B — — — —
School C ·················

Chart 22 Comparison chart for process targets: managing the built environment.

Code	School A						School B						School C				
	Target no. of times, % p.a. or amount	Historic	Comfort	Challenge	Unlikely		Target no. of times, % p.a. or amount	Historic	Comfort	Challenge	Unlikely		Target no. of times, % p.a. or amount	Historic	Comfort	Challenge	Unlikely
O b 1	/																
O b 2																	
O b 3																	
O b 4																	
O b 5																	
O b 6	/ /																
O b 7																	
O b 8																	
O b 9	/																
O b 10																	
O b 11																	

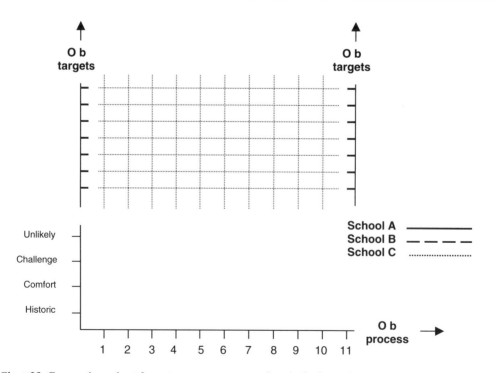

Chart 23 Comparison chart for output targets: managing the built environment.

Code	School A					School B					School C			
	To what extent (0–100%) is this outcome achieved?	Low priority	Mid priority	High priority		To what extent (0–100%) is this outcome achieved?	Low priority	Mid priority	High priority		To what extent (0–100%) is this outcome achieved?	Low priority	Mid priority	High priority
C b 1														
C b 2														
C b 3														
C b 4														
C b 5														
C b 6														
C b 7														
C b 8														
C b 9														
C b 10														
C b 11														

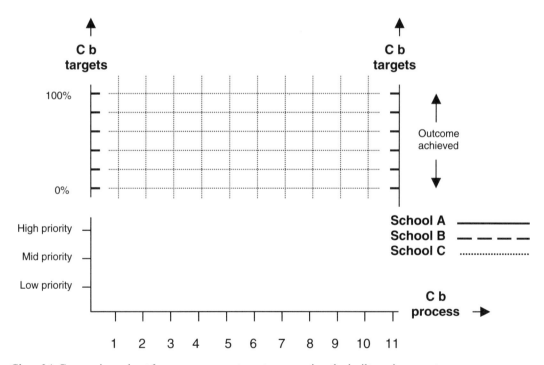

Chart 24 Comparison chart for consequence targets: managing the built environment.

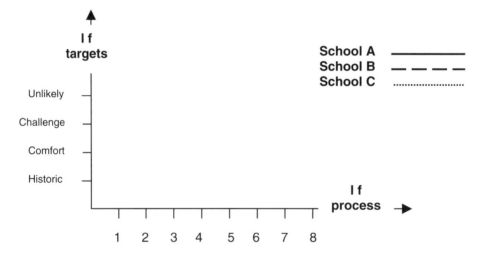

Code	School A					School B					School C			
	Historic	Comfort	Challenge	Unlikely		Historic	Comfort	Challenge	Unlikely		Historic	Comfort	Challenge	Unlikely
I f 1														
I f 2														
I f 3														
I f 4														
I f 5														
I f 6														
I f 7														
I f 8														

Chart 25 Comparison chart for input targets: financial management.

Code	School A						School B						School C				
	Target no. of times, % p.a. or amount	Historic	Comfort	Challenge	Unlikely		Target no. of times, % p.a. or amount	Historic	Comfort	Challenge	Unlikely		Target no. of times, % p.a. or amount	Historic	Comfort	Challenge	Unlikely
P f 1	/																
P f 2	/																
P f 3																	
P f 4																	
P f 5																	
P f 6																	
P f 7																	
P f 8																	

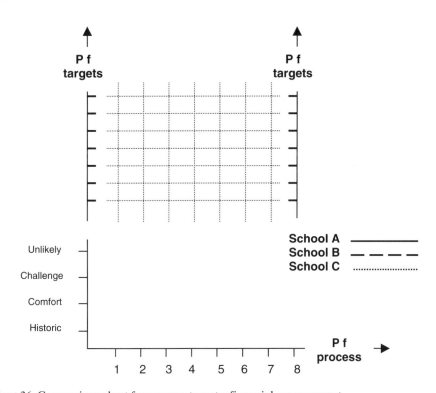

Chart 26 Comparison chart for process targets: financial management.

Code	School A						School B						School C				
	Target no. of times, % p.a. or amount	Historic	Comfort	Challenge	Unlikely		Target no. of times, % p.a. or amount	Historic	Comfort	Challenge	Unlikely		Target no. of times, % p.a. or amount	Historic	Comfort	Challenge	Unlikely
O f 1	/																
O f 2	/																
O f 3	/																
O f 4	/ /																
O f 5																	
O f 6																	
O f 7	/																
O f 8																	

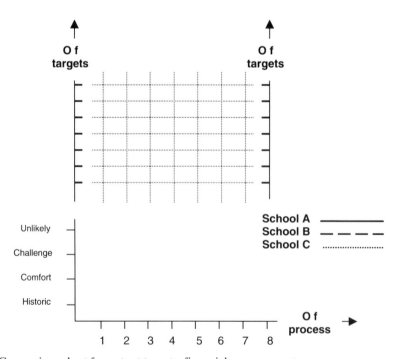

Chart 27 Comparison chart for output targets: financial management.

156

Code	School A					School B					School C			
	To what extent (0–100%) is this outcome achieved?	Low priority	Mid priority	High priority		To what extent (0–100%) is this outcome achieved?	Low priority	Mid priority	High priority		To what extent (0–100%) is this outcome achieved?	Low priority	Mid priority	High priority
C f 1														
C f 2														
C f 3														
C f 4														
C f 5														
C f 6														
C f 7														
C f 8														

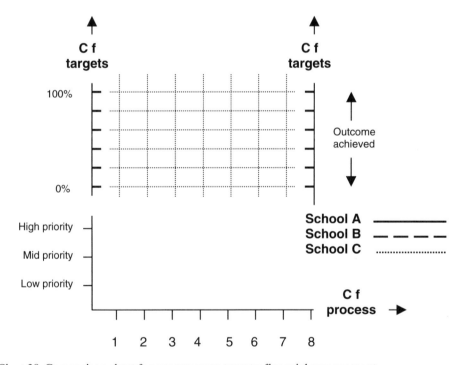

Chart 28 Comparison chart for consequence targets: financial management.

References

Ainscow, M., Hopkins, D., Southworth, G. and West, M. (1994) *Creating the Conditions for School Improvement: a Handbook of Staff Development Activities* (London: David Fulton).

Alexander, R. (1997) *Policy and Practice in Primary Education: Local Initiative, National Agenda* (London: Routledge).

Argyris, C. (1999) *On Organisational Learning* (2nd edition) (Malden, MA: Blackwell).

Barber, M. (1996) *The National Curriculum: A Study in Policy* (Keele: Keele University Press).

Beare, H., Caldwell, B. and Millikan, R. (1997) 'Dimensions of leadership', in *Leadership and Teams in Educational Management*, M. Crawford, L. Kydd and C. Riches (eds) (Buckingham: Open University Press).

Bennett, N. (1992) *Managing Learning in the Primary Classroom* (APSE Paper No. 1) (Stoke: Trentham Books).

Bennis, W. and Nanus, B. (1985) *Leaders: the Strategies for Taking Charge* (New York: Harper & Row).

Bowring-Carr, C. and West-Burnham, J. (1997) *Effective Learning in Schools: How to Integrate Learning and Leadership for a Successful School* (London: Pitman).

Bridges, E. M. (1992) *The Incompetent Teacher: Managerial Responses* (London: Falmer Press).

Burns, J. M. (1978) *Leadership* (New York: Harper and Row).

Bush, T. (2000) 'Management styles: impact on finance and resources', in *Managing Finance and Resources in Education*, M. Coleman and L. Anderson (eds) (London: Paul Chapman).

Coleman, M. and Briggs, A. J. R. (2000) 'Management of Buildings and Space', in *Managing Finance and Resources in Education*, M. Coleman and L. Anderson (eds) (London: Paul Chapman).

Coleman, M., Bush, T. and Glover, D. (1994) *Managing Finance and External Relations* (Harlow: Longman).

Creemers, B. P. M. (1994) *The Effective Classroom* (London: Cassell).

Davies, L. (1997) 'The rise of the school effectiveness movement', in *Perspectives on School Effectiveness and School Improvement*, J. White and M. Barber (eds) (London: University of London Institute of Education).

Deming, W. E. (1986) (19th edition, 1994) *Out of the Crisis: Quality, Productivity and Competitive Position* (Cambridge: Cambridge University Press).

DfEE (1997a) *Setting Targets for Pupil Achievement: Guidance for Governors* (London: DfEE).

DfEE (1997b) *From Targets to Action: Guidance to Support Effective Target-setting in Schools* (London: DfEE).

Drucker, P. (1993) *Post-Capitalist Society* (Oxford: Butterworth Heinemann).

Dubin, R. (1961) *Human Relations in Administration* (Englewood Cliffs, NJ: Prentice-Hall).

Edmonds, R. R. (1981) 'Making public schools effective', *Social Policy*, Vol. 12, pp. 56–60.

Fiedler, F. E. (1967) *A Theory of Leadership Effectiveness* (New York: McGraw-Hill).

Fullan, M. G. (1991) *The New Meaning of Educational Change* (London: Cassell).

Gann, N. (1999) *Targets for Tomorrow's Schools* (London: Falmer Press).

Gardner, H. (1996) *Leading Minds: an anatomy of leadership* (London: HarperCollins).

Good, T. L. and Brophy, J. E. (1986) 'School Effects', in *Handbook of Research on Teaching*, M. Wittrock (ed.) (New York: Macmillan).

Hargreaves, D. H. (1997) 'School culture, school effectiveness and school improvement', in *Organisational Effectiveness and Improvement in Education*, A. Harris, N. Bennett and M. Preedy (eds) (Buckingham: Open University Press).

Hastings, C. (1993) *The New Organisation* (London: McGraw-Hill).

Hersey, P. and Blanchard, K. (1982) *Management of Organisational Behaviour: Utilising Human Resources* (Englewood Cliffs, NJ: Prentice-Hall).

Hopkins, D., Ainscow, M. and West, M. (1994) *School Improvement in an Era of Change* (London: Cassell).

Hutton, R. and Zairi, M. (1994) 'D2D: a quality winner's approach to benchmarking', *International Journal for Quality Management and Technology*, Vol. 1, No. 3, pp. 21–38.

Jackson, D. S. (2000) 'The school improvement journey: perspectives on leadership', *School Leadership and Management*, Vol. 20, No. 1, pp. 61–78.

Jaques, E. (1956) *Measurement of Responsibility: A Study of Work, Payment and Individual Capacity* (London: Tavistock).

Kanter, R. M. (1983) *The Change Masters: Innovation for Productivity in the American Corporation* (New York: Simon & Schuster).

Kelly, A., West, M. and Dee, L. (2001) 'Staff involvement in the design of a key skills curriculum model', *The Curriculum Journal*, Vol. 12, No. 2.

Levacic, R. (1995) *Local Management of Schools: Analysis and Practice* (Buckingham: Open University Press).

Levine, D. U. and Lezotte, L. W. (1990) *Unusually Effective Schools: A Review and Analysis of Research and Practice* (Madison, WI: National Centre for Effective Schools Research and Development).

Lezotte, L. W. (1989) 'School improvement based on the effective schools research', *International Journal of Educational Research*, Vol. 13, No. 7, pp. 815–25.

Louis, K. S. and Miles, M. B. (1990) *Improving the Urban High School: What Works and Why* (New York: Teachers College Press).

Macbeath, J. (1999) *Schools Must Speak for Themselves* (London: Routledge).

McAleese, K. (2000) 'Budgeting in schools', in *Managing Finance and Resources in Education*, M. Coleman and L. Anderson (eds) (London: Paul Chapman).

Mortimore, P., Sammons, P., Stoll, L., Lewis, D. and Ecob, R. (1988) *School Matters: The Junior Years* (Wells: Open Books).

Murgatroyd, S. J. and Morgan, C. (1993) *Total Quality Management and the School* (Buckingham: Open University Press).

Qualification and Curriculum Authority (QCA) (1997) *Target Setting and Benchmarking in Schools: Consultation Paper* (London: QCA).

Reich, R. B. (1987) 'Entrepreneurship reconsidered: the team as hero', *Harvard Business Review*, May–June.

—— (1991) *The Work of Nations: Preparing Ourselves for Twenty-first Century Capitalism* (London: Simon & Schuster).

Reynolds, D. (1976) 'The delinquent school', in *The Process of Schooling: A Sociological Reader*, M. Hammersley and P. Woods (eds) (London: Routledge & Kegan Paul).

Reynolds, D., Creemers, B., Nesselrodt, P., Schaffer, E., Stringfield, S. and Teddlie, C. (1994) *Advances in School Effectiveness Research and Practice* (Oxford: Pergammon).

Reynolds, D. and Murgatroyd, S. (1977) 'The sociology of schooling and the absent pupil: the school as a factor in the generation of truancy', in *Absenteeism in South Wales: Studies of Pupils, Their Homes, and Their Secondary Schools*, H. C. M. Carroll (ed.) (Swansea: University of Swansea Faculty of Education).

Reynolds, D. and Teddlie, C. (2000) 'The processes of school effectiveness', in *The International Handbook of School Effectiveness Research*, C. Teddlie and D. Reynolds (London: Falmer Press).

Rutter, M., Maughan, B., Mortimore, P. and Ouston, J. with Smith, A. (1979) *Fifteen Thousand Hours: Secondary Schools and Their Effects on Children* (London: Open Books).

Sammons, P., Hillman, J. and Mortimore, P. (1995) *Key Characteristics of Effective Schools: A Review of School Effectiveness Research* (London: Institute of Education University of London).

Sammons, P., Thomas, S. and Mortimore, P. (1997) *Forging Links: Effective Schools and Effective Departments* (London: Paul Chapman).

Sawhney, M. and Parikh, D. (2001) 'Where value lives in a networked world', *Harvard Business Review*, Vol. 79, No. 1, pp. 79–86.

Scheerens, J. (1992) *Effective Schooling: Research, Theory and Practice* (London: Cassell).

Scott, W. R. (1997) 'Organisational effectiveness', in *Organisational Effectiveness and Improvement in Education*, A. Harris, N. Bennett and M. Preedy (eds) (Buckingham: Open University Press).

Senge, P. M. (1990) *The Fifth Discipline: The Art and Practice of The Learning Organisation* (London: Century Business).

——(1999) *The Dance of Change: The Challenges to Sustaining Momentum in Learning Organisations* (London: Nicholas Brealey).

Sergiovanni, T. J. (1992) *Moral Leadership: Getting to the Heart of School Improvement* (San Francisco: Jossey-Bass).

Simkins, T. (1998) 'Autonomy, constraint and the strategic management of resources', in *Strategic Management in Schools and Colleges*, D. Middlewood and J. Lumby (eds) (London: Paul Chapman).

Stogdill, R. M. and Bass, B. M. (1981) *Stogdill's Handbook of Leadership: A Survey of Theory and Research* (New York: The Free Press).

Stoll, L. and Fink, D. (1994) 'School effectiveness and school improvement: voices from the field', *School Effectiveness and School Improvement*, Vol. 5, No. 2, pp. 149–77.

Stringfield, S. (1994) 'The analysis of large data bases in school effectiveness research', in *Advances in School Effectiveness Research and Practice*, D. Reynolds *et al.* (eds) (Oxford: Pergammon).

Stringfield, S. and Teddlie, C. (1987) 'A time to summarise: six years and three phases of the Louisiana School Effectiveness Study', quoted in *The International Handbook of School Effectiveness Research*, C. Teddlie and D. Reynolds (2000) (London: Falmer Press).

Teddlie, C. and Stringfield, S. (1993) *Schools Make a Difference: Lessons Learned From a 10-Year Study of School Effects* (New York: Teachers College Press).

Thomas, H. and Martin, J. (1996) *Managing Resources for School Improvement: Creating a Cost-effective School* (London: Routledge).

Tizard, B., Blatchford, P., Burke, J., Farquhar, C. and Plewis, I. (1988) *Young Children at School in the Inner City* (Hove: Lawrence Erlbaum).

Whitehouse, I. and Busher, H. (1990) 'Teachers' views on teaching in a large split-site junior school', *Educational Management and Administration*, Vol. 18, No. 1, pp. 54–60.

Zairi, M. (1996) *Effective Benchmarking: Learning From the Best* (London: Chapman & Hall).

Recommended reading

Camp, R. C. (1989) *Benchmarking: The Search for Best Practices that Lead to Superior Performance* (White Plains, NJ: Quality Press).

Imai, M. (1986) *Kaizen – The Key to Japan's Competitive Success* (New York: McGraw-Hill).

Mortimore, P., Mortimore, J. with Thomas, H. (1994) *Managing Associate Staff: Innovation in Primary and Secondary Schools* (London: Paul Chapman).

Ofsted (1995) *Guidance on the Inspection of Secondary Schools* (London: HMSO).

Pascale, R. T. and Athos, A. G. (1982) *The Art of Japanese Management* (Harmondsworth: Penguin Books).

Index